SELLING ADVERTISING SPACE
IN 90 MINUTES

For a complete list of Management Books 2000 titles
visit our web-site on http://www.mb2000.com

Other titles in the 'in Ninety Minutes' series are:

25 Management Techniques in 90 Minutes
5S Kaizen in 90 Minutes
Active Learning in 90 Minutes
Become a Meeting Anarchist in 90 Minutes
Budgeting in 90 Minutes
Building a Website Using a CMS in 90 Minutes
Credit Control in 90 Minutes
Damn Clients! in 90 Minutes
Deal With Debt in 90 Minutes
Difficult Decisions Solved in 90 minutes
Effective Media Coverage in 90 Minutes
Emotional Intelligence in 90 Minutes
Faster Promotion in 90 Minutes
Find That Job in 90 Minutes
Funny Business in 90 Minutes
Getting More Visitors to Your Website in 90 Minutes
Learn to Use a PC in 90 Minutes
Networking in 90 Minutes
Payroll in 90 Minutes
Perfect CVs in 90 Minutes
Plan a New Website in 90 Minutes
Practical Negotiating in 90 Minutes
Projects kept Simple in 90 Minutes
Run a Successful Conference in 90 Minutes
Strengths Coaching in 90 Minutes
Supply Chain in 90 Minutes
Telling People in 90 Minutes
Understand Accounts in 90 Minutes
Working Together in 90 Minutes

SELLING ADVERTISING SPACE

in 90 Minutes

Brian Neil

2000

First published in 2009 by Management Books 2000 Ltd
Forge House, Limes Road
Kemble, Cirencester
Gloucestershire, GL7 6AD, UK
Tel: 0044 (0) 1285 771441
Fax: 0044 (0) 1285 771055
Email: info@mb2000.com
Web: www.mb2000.com

British Library Cataloguing in Publication Data is available

ISBN 9781852525811

Acknowledgements

Special thanks to all the staff at Centaur Media plc for their support, to Mark Heineman for working to create competencies related to the function of selling advertising space, and to the History of Advertising Trust (www.hatads.org.uk) for very kindly supplying the illustrations and additional historical information.

Contents

Foreword

by Annie Swift
Chief Executive Officer, Institute of Sales Promotion

This is a book on selling. The type of book that abounds the business press sections of libraries and books stores countrywide. The type of book that, when read, immediately reminds us of all the things we know we should be doing to persuade and influence a customer to buy from us. The type of book that makes us feel pleasure because we can say we know all of this, even on a basic level, or that it's quite obvious really, while simultaneously making us feel guilty because we don't actually do it.

Yet with this particular book on selling, there is a difference.

What Brian has managed to do is strike an impressive balance between not taking any of it too seriously while maintaining the valid point that without structure, there can be no sale. He explains it simply, allowing clarity to prevail while seasoning it with the wit and wisdom of many years in the sales saddle. This book presented to me something much more than just another sales tome. It is presented in a context that to my knowledge is not available anywhere else. I am not about to declare that selling media advertisement space is harder or easier than other products because it isn't, but I would say it is different in one very important way – you're not actually selling anything you can touch. This also makes buying it harder as well. The questions raised are: what is it, how much of it do I get, and what is the value? Then the final and most interesting question: how do I know it's been worthwhile buying? Therefore selling media space does need a very distinct type of approach, and to have a book that explains how to do something in a specific industry is now, and forever will be, an absolute gem.

Sales books in general seem to remind me about what isn't being done in sales teams or where to look for flaws in people's approach to selling rather than how to do something better. This is another area where I think this book stands out. It provides the information in a hopeful way. By this I mean it seems to have a stream through which runs a constant message of positive approbation about the primary function of persuasive interaction. The message is that it can be done and be done well! While at the same time it says, 'If you don't like the idea – that's ok too!' It's about knowing more, before commitment is made. Getting things like this right in the first place is really important, as Brian points out.

I think this book should be compulsory reading for media sales managers too. The reason is quite simply that, in order to get the best from a sales team, you need to know what you're looking for both in terms of recruitment and ongoing development. This book will inform even the most experienced and successful media salespeople who have been promoted to manager, what it is they are actually doing. This might appear crazy, but often naturally gifted salespeople are unable to explain to others what they need to do to become as successful. It explains why they're so good and enables them to pass this wisdom onto junior sales staff with clarity and reassurance. In other words, in publishing this book, Brian has provided the raw material for media sales training courses in every English speaking country in the world. Generosity defined.

I've read this book and would do so again. I'd buy a copy for every media sales manager I know and every salesperson and get them to read it too. It is essential reading particularly at the moment when advertising revenues have been so affected by the credit crunch. Never before has it been so important to get the right people in the right jobs, doing it to the right way. In this fantastic 90 minutes series, media sales departments finally have a resource devoted entirely to them.

Such a clever idea and about time.

Annie Swift

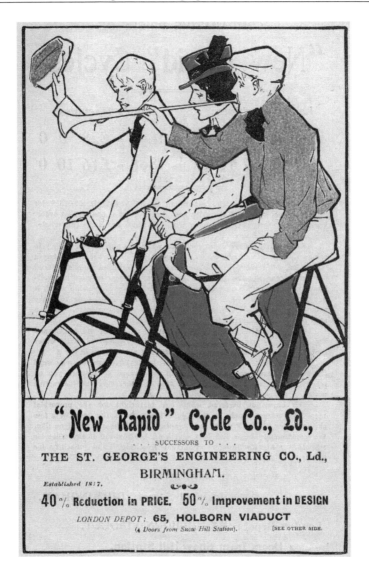

A fabulous example that reflects the excitement of the age around this new mode of transport aimed clearly at both sexes. The New Rapid Cycle Company was based in Birmingham and this advertisement appeared in various consumer print magazines around 1898. The company existed between 1897 and 1904.

Part 1

Introduction

"Courage is what it takes to stand up and speak.
Courage is also what it takes to sit down and listen."

Winston Churchill

1. Why read this book?

Whether you are a college leaver, bored with your current role and in need of a stimulating career, or already working in telesales and needing a reminder of what a media salesperson should be doing, this book will help. It will also be particularly handy during this recession because it explains the structure of an effective sale and puts it in context with the current economic climate. I wrote it because anyone considering media sales, as indeed any other career, should be in possession of a few facts before they decide. Or as a friend says – 'know where the fish are before you put your line in.'

Briefly, media salespeople are responsible for generating revenue through the sale of advertisement space usually for either a magazine or website. They generally work in teams, contacting prospects by phone.

As a professional trainer in a very successful publishing company, I see a great many people entering media sales with only a very limited understanding of the nuances of the role. In some cases, the alleged glamour of 'working in media' allures the freshman to take up the role with the reality of the day-to-day remaining a mystery until the commitment has been made. Others take the role because it simply offers an opportunity to earn a fair salary relatively quickly to pay off student debts, while some decide to get into it because they have been told they are 'good with people', whatever that means.

Publishing houses tend rely on recruitment agencies to source candidates for their media sales departments. It should be a combined effort between the publishing house and agency to establish the key competencies sought and to agree the methods by which they can measure potential candidates. The majority of media recruitment companies do an excellent job of representing the publishing houses. They have a good grasp of the specific requirements of the positions available. Inevitably, there are a few agencies that put forward distinctly inappropriate candidates, persuading both client and candidate they are well suited.

Equally, there are publishing houses that are less than scientific in the recruitment process. Some rely too heavily on the agency to advise them on who they should appoint; some fall back on their own intuition; others leave an inexperienced manager to make the appointment. Some candidates are lured by the promise of continuous training, working in exciting and growing industries, or by the offer of high, often totally unrealistic, 'on-target earnings'. In some cases, the targets are so far away from reality that no one will ever earn the quantity of money promised. I have seen many failed probations, early resignations and low personal revenue levels, which are a direct result of poor recruitment. While interviews are never going to prove conclusively whether or not the individual is right for a role in media sales, more can be done to ensure mistakes are avoided. It is the responsibility of the agent, putting the candidate forward, the recruiting manager and indeed the individual to work out if there is a fit.

I think a fair proportion of those entering media sales at this level consider the role a stepping stone to greater things and indeed the skills learned in this job do offer an excellent foundation for the future. However, this is hardly the best reason to make what may be the most important decision of your life.

Many university-leavers are desperate to get a job as quickly as they can – too quickly, in some cases. It is true that a degree today does not mean the same to employers as it did 20 years ago (when the percentage of the population going through university was far smaller), and with huge numbers of graduates pouring into the job market every year the competition for jobs is fierce. The situation is exacerbated by the financial burden brought on by student loans. The result is that many take the first job they can find.

Some students seem to think the work has been done, and they don't need to worry too much about the next step: now all that needs to happen is the career, followed by a gazelle-like leap into management, then, a couple of lunches later, a board position and finally early retirement in Tahiti.

However, life for our newly crowned youngsters is more complicated and, despite having worked very hard under a great deal of pressure for years, there is simply no fast track to anything. In fact the worst move you can make is to take a job for the sake of it and

16

see what happens. I admit that for university leavers, media sales does present itself as an attractive and accessible option and if you have to rush, then do so but with better information so at least you know what it's all about. Bad decisions are frequently made as a result of a lack of information and I admit during my career I have had to rush into jobs for one reason or another and have made the odd mistake. With hindsight, I wouldn't necessarily have done things differently but at least I would have gone into them more prepared.

The other problem, of course, is the current social preoccupation with instant gratification. I may risk sounding old but because children have a CD player, an iPod and a mobile phone by the time they are two and a half, the currency of life's little pleasures to be earned and enjoyed as we progress is diluted by the scourge of immediate fulfilment. My theory is that it all started with Wash & Go shampoo, or pre-cut apples. We have become addicted to reaching the destination without enjoying the journey that gets us there. When I find myself waiting for lifts, it often happens that as people join me they press the button to call for the lift despite it being lit in glowing red to assure them the lift is on its way. I have seen people become irritated by the amount of time it takes for some websites to appear, which is astonishing if you think about it. Before we had the internet, we had to look things up in the library, which involved far greater involvement and patience. Developing commercial skills takes time but it is without doubt a very worthwhile investment of time.

Just as a footnote to this section, my nightmare is that our children's children, on being asked to draw some fruit, will draw a semi-circular segment, coloured in Euro standard green, wrapped in a plastic bag and call it an apple. Another concern I have is whether or not Wash & Go is compulsory. I mean, if you decide you don't want to 'go', is that acceptable, or should you choose another shampoo?

I do, however, have a genuine concern that new recruits I meet believe they have learned a great deal already and now it's time to begin reaping the rewards. I often hear of disappointment from those six months into the job of media sales regarding the lack of opportunity to progress their careers. The reality is everyone has to work very hard for relatively little for quite a while before life becomes more comfortable.

Perhaps employers are partly to blame for the belief that fast-track careers exist and maybe in some industries they do. The important fact here is to know what you're getting into before you get into it and take time to learn the craft. Being good at something takes experience and you can't get pre-cut 'experience' in a plastic bag... yet.

2. What is selling?

I began my career in media as a motorcycle messenger for an advertising agency in London. Following a year or so at that, I got a job at Harlech Television selling the space that occurs between programmes on commercial channels. I stayed with Harlech for about 18 months before accepting an offer to become a media buyer for another advertising agency. I was then on the receiving end of the types of calls I had been making only weeks before. I mention this because, as a buyer, I have to admit to developing a sense of superiority over the sellers because I had both the money to spend and the power to choose. It was only later that I learned a good salesperson builds a sale on two fundamental principles. The first is that people will buy more from people they like and respect. The second is that you must ensure the value of the product is clear before trying to do a deal. It is the application of these two principles that levels the playing field between buyer and seller and restricts the choices available to the buyer because they see your product as the only one that can truly match their needs.

If the buyer sees why one product is superior, there is greater likelihood of them buying. It requires a combination of personality, structure and persuasion. These three factors are as important to a barrister or the Prime Minister as they are to a salesperson and yet, for some reason, selling has failed to develop fully as an honourable career. If you asked me what I did for a living and I said that I persuaded people to see things from my perspective through knowledge of the subject, a sound structure and a honed communication style, would you think I was a barrister, business guru, teacher, policeman or salesperson? These are undoubtedly the skills of life, highly transferable and an extremely valuable asset. Good selling involves being able to forge relationships with a diverse range of personalities, knowing the product being sold inside out and being a problem solver.

There is an ever-increasing volume of educational courses in the UK for business folk to develop their communication skills. These courses teach people how to understand human motivation, be more influential, change opinion and persuade, all of which are the working tools of a salesperson. Someone said once that 'business starts when someone sells something.' The something can be anything from a product to a person, from ideas to inspiration.

Selling media space at entry level can involve making up to 100 calls a day to clients who take many calls from salespeople and often have no wish to indulge in any type of conversation. It is by nature repetitive and full of rejection, but nonetheless offers a good framework for developing interpersonal and communication skills.

Selling is about influencing others. No one can force someone else to do something (unless you own a gun, naturally) but we can use our own belief in a solution to persuade others that our ideas are worthy of consideration through logical and well-reasoned argument. Some current telephone 'marketing' operations, such as those that phone us at home with recorded messages, perpetuate the myth that selling is a second-class occupation. Salespeople who smother customers with too much product information or appear too eager or simply stand too close, also give the business of selling a bad name. Selling is the ability to flex our methods of communication so our approach appeals to the majority. It is the art of listening to others and having enough genuine interest to understand and solve problems. It is the skill of spotting prospects, building rapport and closing deals and always being hungry for more, all of which are dealt with in more detail later on.

Another classic advertisement that captures the era. First published around 1899 as a monthly and continued for many years. This was a 'quality' boy's magazine which featured ripping yarns of derring-do, the adventures of the school hero and suchlike boys own editorial. Contributors included John Buchan and P.G. Wodehouse.

Part 2

How we got to where we are today

"Four hostile newspapers are more to be feared than a thousand bayonets."

Napoleon Bonaparte

3. Printing & publishing – a brief history

William Caxton is often hailed as the inventor of the printing press but in fact it was Johannes Gutenberg who, 20 years earlier in 1436, first began production on a wooden printing device. This required craftsmen to cut away the background leaving the raised lettering and illustration. This process was extremely costly and time-consuming, and the output was inevitably limited to the tiny proportion of the population who had the finance and education to enjoy it. In those days, the books produced were, unsurprisingly, religious in nature and written in Latin. The introduction of metal type in 1455 began the revolution that was to lead to one of main growth industries of the century. By the early 1500s, printing had become established in most of Europe, and Britain was once again leading the way.

With the arrival of a large number of plague-ridden rats in the mid-1600s, the Royal Court abandoned London and fled to Oxford – a move which provoked a feeling of abandonment by London's general public. It was in Oxford that Charles II granted Henry Muddiman permission to produce a paper called *The Oxford Gazette,* with the aim of publishing information the Royal Court felt appropriate – representing an early form of press release. In this respect it could be argued that publishing started life as a result of a general breakdown in Royal PR (still a source of much editorial copy today). The paper had much broader appeal than was imagined, mainly being used by business owners of the day to keep tabs on the unrest across the land and to protect their business interests and personal wealth. (While King Charles laundered his wig collection, he remained unaware of the potential of this idea. He would never know that this was the embryo of an industry that in 2008 had a turnover of around £15 billion.)

Once London had recovered from the plight of disease and the Royal family had returned to the city, *The London Gazette* was launched. It continued as a periodical reporting accurate information of relevance from a Royal perspective. In 1785 it was joined by the

Daily Universal Register, which brought outrage, humour and scandal through text and illustration into the public domain. Its colourful and absorbing accounts of popular life in the 1790s appealed to a much wider audience; it went on to become *The Times.*

The London Gazette is still published today and represents official government information, public notices, town and country planning and, interestingly, notice of anyone requesting permission for expeditions to Antarctica.

Printing and publishing continued to flourish and by the end of the 17th century there were 150 paper mills in the UK employing 2,500 workers. Needless to say, this was to grow substantially over the next two centuries. One of the world's oldest publications, catering for those in the shipping and insurance industry, was *Lloyd's List,* first published in 1734.

As the printing and publishing industries prospered, there was a parallel social movement. People were beginning to want to know more. With the excitement and opportunity that the industrial revolution created, information was becoming the bedrock of commerce. Business leaders wanted information on their markets, their competitors, law and finance and they looked to the publishing industry to provide it. The 1850s saw the emergence of giant printing presses that were capable of handling large print runs relatively cost effectively. National and regional papers were beginning to infiltrate 19th-century society along with greetings cards, maps and advertisements.

Business and trade magazines also began to appear. A magazine called *The Engineer* was launched in 1856 aiming to provide a mix of news and analysis of emerging technologies, innovations and applications across the sector. That was 150 years ago, and the magazine still exists today and is stronger than ever.

The UK's oldest consumer magazine, *The Field,* was launched in 1853 and is still a wonderful publication. Several more decades passed before women got their own magazine – *The Lady,* which launched in 1885, was the UK's first weekly for women, and that too is still lauded as a very fine publication today.

While clearly catering for very different markets, the commonality is that all these periodicals needed funding and the two main revenue streams were copy sales and advertisement space. The business of selling advertising therefore was at the heart of commerce from the very beginning. The sale of advertising space made an enormous contribution to creating and sustaining the publishing industry as it does today. Imagine selling advertising in the 1850s...

Britain was the most powerful and industrially mature country in the world and the prime minister of the day was Lord Palmerston, who took the role in 1855 after a long haul as foreign minister. He was a Conservative prime minister and appeared very interested in increasing Britain's power in Europe, capitalising on the wealth and reputation of the nation. While generally speaking he was a popular leader, he did have his faults, one of which was a fondness for Queen Victoria's ladies in waiting, leading to a telling comment by the old Queen: "I never liked him." Despite his tendency to upset things from time to time, he led the country through one of the most prolific times in British history, and remained in office until he died in 1865 at the age of 81.

The country was undoubtedly enjoying the fruits of its own imagination. There had been plenty of investment and support to make the impossible happen and the world changed as a result. Human existence was revolutionised. Rail travel was becoming quite the norm in the late 1800s but, if you wished to avoid the quite frightening speed of train travel, there was another new invention known as the bicycle. This mode of transport became very fashionable across Britain and was cheap enough for a great many. If nothing else, the bicycle revolutionised female clothing, freeing women from corset imprisonment forever.

The arrival of the steam press increased the demand for pulp fiction, mainly by the lower classes it seemed (some of whom had now been allowed to learn to read) along with a profusion of national and regional newspapers. The Newspapers Proprietors Association was founded in 1906 and the Society of Weekly Newspaper and Periodical Proprietors (now known as the Periodical Publishers Association) were incorporated under the Companies Act of 1908. Despite advertising being prevalent in a vast number of periodicals since the 1850s, an advertisement 'watchdog' wasn't set up until 1962. The Advertising Standards Authority is an independent body set up by the advertising industry to police the rules for advertisements, sales promotions and direct marketing in the UK.

Prior to 1850, press advertisements tended to be sold by the line as opposed to the size, which came in later when magazines were divided into column widths. Mass or national advertising began about this time with the type of products being advertised in consumer publications including washing and cleaning products, musical scores, hair tonics, sauces and prepared food items. In the 1880s furniture was being advertised along with clothing and sewing machines. By the early 1900s advertising was getting more adventurous using images and captions to enhance the effect. Without the benefit of an advertising watchdog, many advertisers made outrageous claims about their product capabilities. Advertisement illustrators were much in demand for their skill at understanding how to depict 'lifestyle' or increase 'brand dominance'. It was the enthusiasm and talent of this fast-growing fraternity that ensured advertisement illustration captured the essence of the brand of the day.

One was Wilfred Moody Fryer (1891-1968), who graduated from Bradford College of Art in 1909. He worked as a freelance illustrator for the advertising industry for many years and particularly enjoyed drawing steam trains and motor cars but also excelled in the more feminine, less industrial elements of society. As well as drawing for advertisements, he created magazine and book covers, showing an immense talent for depicting an advertising message through illustration.

Selling advertising space in the early days of publishing would have been no less important to the business and not much different in terms of process, than today. The primary benefit of buying an advertisement in 1850 would have been to reach a specific type of reader, which is the same as today. The salesperson would have had to persuade through effective communication and explanation that a certain magazine was the best choice in 1850 just as he or she does in 2009. There would have been pressure on the salesperson to achieve revenues, just as in modern publishing houses. How difficult the job of selling advertising was during these times would have depended to some degree on the economy. In 1850, of course, Britain was booming, whereas today there is more competition and perhaps less economic certainty. At least today we don't have to explain the meaning of the word 'advertisement' as they might have had to do back then.

The Periodical Publishers Association (PPA) website states there are more than 8,500 business and consumer magazines published in the UK reflecting a 4.8% growth over the last ten years. There are approximately 700 publishing companies in the UK with 44% of revenues originating from classified advertisement sales.

Online advertising has grown significantly over the last five years. A report from the IAB (Interactive Advertising Bureau) and PricewaterhouseCoopers stated that the online share of the total UK advertising spend has grown from 15.3% in 2007 to 19% in 2008. The UK's online advertising spend is currently over £3b per annum. One hugely successful publishing company has seen online revenues grow from 600k to £16m in eight years. The Association of Online Publishers census supports these results stating that digital publishers have seen a 52% increase in total revenues. Prior to the credit crunch, the prediction was that publishing revenues would climb by 8% during 2009 with digital growth figures reaching 31%. It has been estimated that over the next few years, digital revenues will overtake spending on TV advertising. Although the current economic condition will inevitably slow down online advertising escalation in the short term, the prognosis of rapid and global online advertising growth remains extremely optimistic.

This further indicates the importance of these mediums and the relevance and responsibility of the sales departments. The provenance of selling advertising space in periodicals is distinguished and honourable. It has been the pulse of publishing for nearly two centuries and anyone already involved or considering taking up the mantle of this profession should do so with pride. I should add that while one should be proud to hold a position in advertisement sales, this is not an ingredient that will guarantee success or enjoyment of the job. However, knowing more about the role will reduce the likelihood of making an appalling mistake.

4. Different types of publishers and revenue streams – the modern world

Today, publishing can be split into a number of categories. These include consumer, business-to-business (b2b) and trade. Business-to-business publishing is an information industry generating nearly £15 billion a year in the UK (this includes all revenue areas, not just magazines). The PPA recently reported that business magazines in the UK generate revenues of more than £3.3 billion.

There are also national, international and local newspaper publishing companies, contract publishing houses, book publishers and digital (online) publishers. The commercial publishing industry has a total revenue of about £30 billion and employs around 280,000 people in the UK. As already mentioned, there are 700 companies providing business information in the UK employing about 29,000 people.

It is not unusual for one company to publish a variety of types of product but most tend to have a dominant product type. Consumer publishing houses print and publish entertainment or leisure magazines. Some are of general interest, while others serve more specific niches, such as music, sport or beauty. Magazines such as *FHM*, *Woman's Journal* and *Heat* are typical consumer publications. These provide access to a specific type of reader that represents the advertising company's customers. For example, it may be that a fashion house wishes to reach young, professional, well-educated female adults with a relatively high disposable income, so it should choose to advertise its products in a magazine largely read by this type of individual. It is likely there are a number of magazines that have a readership made up of this group so it is the job of the media salesperson to convince those responsible for buying the advertising space that their publication is best suited to achieving the marketing goal.

All of us, with the possible exception of those inhabiting a desert island, without transport and hundreds of miles from the nearest Debenhams, are influenced by the messages in our environment.

Rather sadly, as a species, we lap it up, proving we have an endless appetite for the banal. Currently, we are being warned to be a little more frugal as a result of a massive increase in consumer spending, yet still the spending escalates. The problem is the influence of those that make products and lifestyle changes easy to attain. The principle of waiting and saving understood by past generations barely exists any more, and the line between needing something and wanting something is distinctly hazy. Consumer advertising has become very perceptive, tapping into our apparent need for, well, everything. Our views and opinions, the way we look, even the way we speak, are influenced by what we see, hear and experience.

Traditionally, trade magazines provided printed information for blue-collar industries such as grocery, manufacturing, retail and construction. Business magazines tended to focus on the running of businesses such as marketing, management and finance. The distinction between trade and business titles has become blurred over the years as many non-consumer publications cover all aspects of a business sector.

Every publishing company has a different way of doing things but, in general, companies that publish to make money require revenues from the sale of advertisement space. This is as true for *The Washington Post* as it is for the *Basildon Evening Echo*, and all of them rely on this primary source of revenue to keep the home fires burning.

Other revenue streams include the sale of subscriptions. A subscription is essentially an up-front payment by a reader for a supply of whichever magazine takes their fancy. It is delivered to the door of the subscriber, often earlier than it is available anywhere else. Although subscriptions are available for consumer magazines too, for a b2b publishing house this arrangement is ideal. It creates a regular and identified readership, which appeals to advertisers and ensures the publishing house receives income up-front. It is an important revenue stream and one that justifies a high level of attention and good maintenance.

In publishing houses, the subscribers are the basis of another important revenue stream, that of list rental. The names of subscribers provide a list of consumers and professionals proven to be active in that market. An advertiser may wish to reach marketing professionals, for example, using two means. The first may be to place an advertisement in a leading b2b publication and the second may be to send out a piece of direct mail to underpin the advertising message. The traditional method of posting a printed flyer is increasingly being replaced by email or e-marketing, which is faster and considerably cheaper.

For a consumer campaign, subscribers are used in a similar way. A company wishing to rent holiday apartments on the Costa del Sizzle may advertise in a lifestyle magazine and then buy a number of additional lists from various list brokers of the same demographic, to support the advertising.

Whatever the method used, a direct mail campaign will require a list that is truly representative of the target audience and minimises the wastage prevalent in many direct mail campaigns. One choice open to the advertiser is to have the mailer sent to the subscribers of a top marketing publication (or a number of publications related to the sector). With this option, he is reassured his mailer is going to be received by those that are interested in marketing solutions as they subscribe to the corresponding magazines. Any magazine that has a high number of subscribers is clearly doing something right and this is recognised by advertisers.

List rental departments can be quite operationally expensive, however, but are important to maintain. Collectively, b2b magazines' news-stand copy sales (through newsagents), subscriptions and list or e-list rental are all highly valuable sources of revenue. Book publishers differ in that generally they do not carry advertising. The revenue is exclusively generated from sales of copies from retail outlets, websites or direct from the publishing house. B2b publishers often produce affiliated products as an additional method to raise revenue. It is common, for example, for a business publisher to own exhibitions, conferences and annual print products that are connected to the industries served. This is helpful from an advertiser's perspective as it offers promotional continuity and a single entry point to networking opportunities within a sector. Consumer publishers also own associated exhibitions and often promote their brands through sponsorship. Essentially, both consumer and b2b publishers try to serve their markets as efficiently as possible and the more efficient they are at doing so, the greater their profitability.

With every profitable market comes increased competition. Inevitably, this makes the job of selling media space or subscriptions more difficult. A publishing house may invest in launching a new product, work hard at growing the advertising market and develop associated products as well as taking all the early financial risk. Once the market is open and it looks like a good bet, other publishers enter the market and launch a competing title. This is all healthy competition, of course, and has occurred in every market since someone invented the word 'compete'.

In any area of publishing, one of the functions of a media salesperson is to be able to differentiate clearly between the products available to the advertisers. (Knowing your competition is on page 1 of any selling manual.) Publishers need to remain inspired thinkers to ensure the optimum revenue is achieved from the markets served. For example, a consumer magazine about home decoration may well have an associated exhibition once a year and perhaps a few special 'spin-off' publications, maybe even a book endorsed by a celebrity as well as a website, ensuring all the commercial bases are covered. Being slow on a commercial opportunity may be a very expensive error as others are often quick to take market share.

Printed magazines also have different frequencies. Whether a magazine is monthly, bi-monthly or weekly is determined by the pace of the market it serves and whether the editorial content is predominantly news or longer feature articles. It is up to the publishing house to determine the frequency according to these criteria. From a financial perspective, it is clearly better to publish more frequently but only if there is enough money in the market to sustain it. Publishing and distributing 52 magazines is clearly more expensive that publishing 12, but the advertisement and subscription sales potential is considerably greater too.

In particular, b2b publications have historically relied on revenue generated from the sale of recruitment advertising space. Job ads appear in the classified sections at the back of most b2b publications and, depending on the market, will represent the largest single contributing section in b2b publishing. Companies advertise available positions within specific sectors as and when they become available. This revenue stream is distinctly volatile for publishing houses owing to the unpredictability of the employment market.

The wiser b2b publishers place their eggs in a variety of baskets, hence the development of other revenue streams such as digital, live events and subscription departments.

*The **LLFIC** was situated at 45 Dale Street Liverpool and had an office in London in the Chancery Lane area. It was established in 1861 and operated successfully for many years and by the look of this advertisement, clearly had a very proactive, if not inspired marketing department. In 1919, it acquired Law Union and Rock Insurance and finally in 1961 the entire company was acquired by Royal Insurance Co.*

Part 3

The (classified) media sales job undressed

"Let the path be open to talent."

Napoleon Bonaparte

5. The job itself

Classification means arranging something according to type, class or category. Classified sections in magazines and newspapers categorise the advertisers' products and services under a variety of headings and place them all at the back so they are easier to find.

Business publications are purchased because they provide readers with relevant sector information that helps them in their work. The advertisements help the reader learn which companies can provide solutions to the issues they face. The reader may contact some of these companies to discuss it further, which could result in a new business relationship. In consumer publishing, classified advertisements usually reflect the likely lifestyle choices of the reader and, again, attempt to lure the consumer into purchase.

The size of advertisements in the classified sections may vary depending on how persuasive the media salesperson has been and the size of the advertiser's budget. It may also depend on how much text they want to include in the advertisement or if they wish to incorporate an illustration or picture. Once sold, each advertisement is then placed under the appropriate section heading and is prepared for publication.

From a commercial perspective, the main purpose for these varied classified sections is to attract new advertisers and to offer them a variety of methods to promote their services or products. In b2b, an 'Appointments' section will carry recruitment advertising. An 'Update' or 'Marketplace' section will encourage companies to advertise their products perhaps with photographs and editorial explanation. A 'Directory' will offer companies – perhaps those unable to afford advertising in any other way – an opportunity to list their contact details and very basic information in the magazine at relatively low cost. 'Business/financial services' sections offer another form of promotion that attracts specific sections of an industry.

If you are selling media advertising space in the classified section of a b2b magazine, it is better to be able to offer a financial services company, for example, the option to advertise in a section with the heading 'Financial services' than to suggest they place their advertisement somewhere in the middle of all the other advertising. Similarly, online publishers can content-match advertising. This means advertisements can be placed close by related editorial content. Users are encouraged to enter key words into the search field and thereby be taken to a page that provides relevant editorial content as well as advertised messages.

From a reader perspective, it is easier and quicker to locate the service or product required if the classified advertising is divided into sections. So everyone wins. B2b websites that are associated to a print magazine version often provide a 'vacancies' section as well that details available jobs in a given industry. This again provides information to the reader that is both useful and easy to locate.

The classified section in a consumer magazine will have a variety of headings to help the reader. In magazines aimed at adults aged 25-34, for example, the classified sections may provide products and services relating to health, diet, beauty or education (or in the case of one I read, clairvoyance and phone-dating). Their associated websites also carry the equivalent classified advertisements to enable advertisers to strengthen their messages and indeed, to help readers access the right product or service for their requirements. (Although, now I come to think of it, clairvoyance could save a bit of time if you're planning to take up phone-dating.).

I have digressed already. This chapter is about the job of selling media advertising space. Space?

Space is the final frontier, we all know that, but how much does it cost? The problem is, if you want to sell space, you are going to have difficulty explaining how you know its value and getting clients to accept your price. If you sell 'access to customers', however, this is more tangible and easier to evaluate. It is also something that potential advertisers actually want. While they may like space and have a smouldering desire to help Captain Kirk discover it, they may not actually want to buy it.

As an entry-level media sales executive working for a publisher, you would normally work as part of a telesales team and report to the advertisement or telesales manager. Your responsibilities include generating a preset volume of revenue. This will require you to make a predetermined number of calls each day to a client-base of existing and potential advertisers that is usually provided for you.

The clients you call will range from those that are friendly, positive and proactive advertisers that value your offer to those that have never advertised, dislike the prospect of doing so and are wary of salespeople. Hopefully, the former will prevail, but whoever they are and whatever their view, your job is to call them and sell them as much advertising as possible. Simple really! Success is dependent on a number of factors, not least of which is the strength of the publication. More on this later.

The job itself can be reviewed by looking at the role profile. The section below outlines the key requirements that most publishing houses look for in their salespeople.

Key performance indicators (KPIs)

These are the factors by which your ability to do the job will be measured, including:

- Performance against predetermined and agreed sales targets.
- Yield (the rate at which each advertisement is sold compared with target).
- Market share (how the volume of advertisements and revenue of your section compares with rival publications).
- Call rates (in most companies telesales managers monitor the number of calls made by their team – the expectation varies from market to market and from magazine to magazine but you should reckon to make about 60 outgoing calls a day).

Key competencies

A competency is an attribute or skill that is required to be able to do the job effectively. The job of media advertisement sales may require some or all of the following **attributes**:

Adaptability

Adaptability is being flexible and working effectively within a variety of situations and with various individuals or groups. It includes the versatility to undertake a variety of tasks while meeting deadlines.

Where demonstrated in the role:

- Adapting the approach to suit the customer.
- Thinking on your feet and demonstrating mental agility.
- Being able to speak to a wide variety of different people at different levels.
- Managing your time to make calls across various services.
- Adopting a structured approach to deal with complaints.
- Being able to structure the sales call.
- Meeting deadlines.

(Very few of us will have all these competencies. Time management, for example, is a skill we can develop or be trained in.)

Enthusiasm

An enthusiastic attitude implies the ability to remain upbeat, think positively and not be deflected by adversity.

Where demonstrated in the role:

- Convincing people of the value to their business of what you are selling.
- Sounding interesting and interested when on the phone.
- Treating the call as unique and not the 59th in a long day.

Initiative

Initiative is a bias for action, proactively doing things and not simply *thinking* about future actions.

Where demonstrated in the role:

- Finding out who to speak to.
- Being creative in your approach to generating sales.
- Identifying and chasing leads.

(**Lead chasing** is a term referring to the activity of searching for new prospective and as yet unknown clients. 'New leads' are often found by looking through competitive publications.)

Inquisitiveness

Inquisitiveness is driven by an underlying curiosity and desire to know more about things, people or issues. It may include 'digging' or pressing for exact information and resolution of discrepancies by asking a series of questions.

Where demonstrated in the role:

- Understanding how a client's business works.
- Being interested in the client's business.
- Spotting the opportunity for new sales.

(Questions are particularly important and covered later in the book)

Motivation

Motivation involves the willingness to apply oneself to work without being distracted, or finding reasons to swerve from achieving goals and objectives. It also includes the motivation to be competitive and to want to be recognised for doing a good job and being successful.

Where demonstrated in the role:

- Making the required number of calls per day.
- Chasing leads (potential customers).
- Exceeding targets set.
- Being seen to want to progress your career.

Resilience/persistence
Resilience is the ability to stick with a difficult task over an extended period when faced with obstacles or rejection. It includes the ability to handle and manage pressure, while remaining positive and enthusiastic.

Where demonstrated in the role:

- Not being put off by rejection or rudeness and maintain motivation.
- Keeping on trying to contact the decision-maker.
- Overcoming objections.

(Specific objections, such as 'it's too expensive' or 'we didn't get any response', are discussed later in the book.)

In addition to the attributes listed above, specific **skills** will be required in the following areas:

Communication – verbal and written
Communication refers to the ability to use active listening techniques, ask appropriate questions and give feedback, and apply an appropriate level of style and tone while interacting with customers. It also includes the ability to express oneself in a variety of interesting and imaginative ways.

Written communication refers to the ability to express information and ideas clearly and concisely through the use of an appropriate written medium. This includes the ability to interpret and apply the written word using spelling, grammar and expression at an appropriate level.

Where demonstrated in the role:

- Being articulate and flexible with the ability to express oneself in a variety of imaginative and creative ways to overcome objections.

- Being direct and precise in conversational style and focusing on what is important in a limited time.
- Being able to ask logical probing questions.
- Listening carefully to find out client needs.
- Being prepared to listen to advice.
- Writing proposals.

Customer care

Customer care is a desire to help or serve others to meet their needs. It means focusing one's efforts on discovering and meeting the customer's needs.

Where demonstrated in the role:

- Proposing alternative solutions to client issues.
- Maintaining client contact.
- Building rapport to sell services.
- Paying attention to detail to get things right first time.
- Solving service problems.
- Displaying necessary urgency to remedy problems.

Negotiation

Negotiation skills include the ability to achieve an acceptable outcome for both parties in a sales situation. This includes application of an acceptable process to achieve an outcome that is in the best interests of both the customer and company.

Where demonstrated in the role:

- Striving to find a solution appropriate for both parties.
- Understanding the needs of the other, while working towards achieving the objectives of the company.
- Using known variables to negotiate to protect price.

(While this is indeed a very important competency, it is unlikely school leavers will have had much experience in negotiation, so many companies offer training in this area.)

Numeracy
Numeracy is the ability to work with numbers to perform various types of calculation including addition, multiplication, division and subtraction. This may also include the ability to perform calculations to effect basic commercial transactions.

Where demonstrated in the role:

- Calculating percentages.
- Generating comparative figures.
- Assessing market share.
- Keeping the books.

Teamwork
Teamwork is the ability to work co-operatively with others, to be part of a team working together rather than demonstrating a preference for working in isolation.

Where demonstrated in the role:

- Being aware of others problems.
- Being considerate.
- Being thoughtful to others.
- Having a desire to achieve team goals.
- Sharing knowledge with other members of the team.
- Being prepared to socialise with or help others.

At interview, a good recruiting manager or agency will look for evidence of the above competencies or at least the potential for them to exist. It may be the case that the particular skill or competency that is not evident can be attended to through training once you join the company (if training is offered).

It is important not to be put off by the list of competencies. You don't have to see your entire personality reflected in them but if you didn't feel an element of excitement when reading through, you may like to keep an open mind!

Not every publishing house seeks the same competencies. It depends on the product and selling environment. The above list is merely an indication of the types of abilities under scrutiny at the majority of media sales interviews. In some instances, sales interviews are competency based, which means the employer is clear on which skill or ability they seek and will conduct interviews to determine if the candidates possess the requisite talents.

6. Career prospects

Think of working as a media sales executive as an apprenticeship to a life in business. This role is not just rewarding from a job satisfaction and remuneration perspective; it is also an investment you are making in yourself. Those who stick at it are opening doors to their futures. The two most crucial skills you need in business are being able to communicate at all levels and being generally commercially minded. Being equipped with these skills will ensure you manage to achieve more with the help and support of others and make money at the same time. You begin learning these skills when you join a company as a media sales executive.

In publishing the career route is along the lines illustrated in the following diagram set out on page 49.

The precise layout will vary depending on the type of publishing house. For national newspaper publishers the Telesales Department is likely to be much larger, with staff working on a variety of different products with display located elsewhere.

The diagram is illustrative of a typical consumer or b2b arrangement and demonstrates that (**classified**) **media sales executive** is the entry point. Depending on the size of the business, you may be able to graduate to a senior position on the team and then perhaps transfer to a display role. Display sales executives are responsible for the larger corporate advertisements placed throughout the printed publication or the larger advertisements on a website such as the ones found on home pages. Display executives sell on the phone and also arrange and attend meetings presenting the product to prospective clients. The next rung on the ladder is perhaps helping to run an advertisement sales team or having sole responsibility for a sales team. In larger teams there may also be an advertisement director, who has overall responsibility for both teams and reports directly to the publisher.

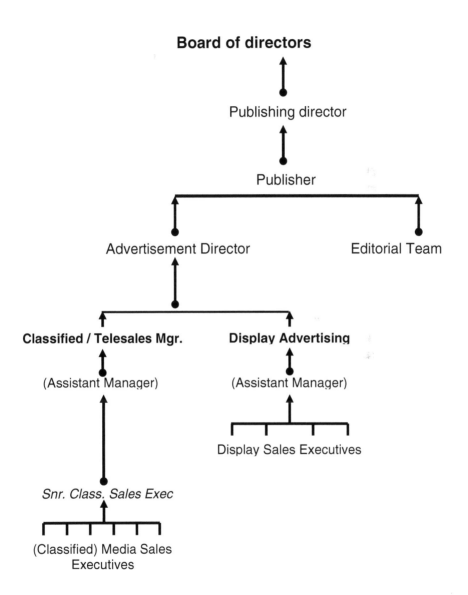

From a career perspective, it is looking good. There has never been more opportunity for media sales executives to develop their careers. Career progression and sales specialisation is on offer with the development of online publishing. In many cases, the commercial success of online has justified an Online Sales Manager and specific online sales staff to be recruited in addition to existing sales teams. This obviously provides another area of opportunity for those wishing to climb the ladder or expand their skill repertoire. I should make the point that in some companies, sales teams are being provided with re-training in Portfolio Sales or Cross Platform Selling. This is to enable existing sales staff to sell across a number of different media which may include offering traditional print advertisement sales opportunities as well as online, special supplements, display and even sponsorship to single clients. If a client is interested in buying a smaller advertisement for example, it would be entirely appropriate for a portfolio salesperson to try and interest them in a number of other opportunities to enable the client to achieve their marketing aims.

Following a sales career, the opportunity extends to becoming a publisher. These are the people responsible for the profitability of the magazine. They handle all print and paper purchasing deals, develop new products, manage the senior staff in the editorial and advertising departments and take charge of key account management. They will also have a significant responsibility for the circulation and marketing of the product or products and be involved with brand positioning via live events such as exhibitions and conferences.

There are a great many individuals currently running UK publishing houses who began in junior media sales jobs. In one major publishing company I know of, some 44% of the board of directors, 67% of the sales managers and a very large proportion of publishers started at entry-level media sales earlier in their careers.

Not only is it more cost effective for publishing houses to recruit from within but it also makes a great deal of sense from the point of continuity.

Those that get promoted will have proved themselves as effective salespeople. They will have demonstrated company loyalty; they will have got to know the markets and how that particular business operates. These individuals are a known quantity and if they are keen to progress, will almost certainly be given the opportunity to do so.

If there is one thing I can guarantee it is that, if you are unsure about career options, this is one opportunity not to be dismissed and can offer an extremely good living.

7. Salary levels

The IDS Executive Compensation Review for graduate pay and progression for the second half of this decade, states that earnings for graduates ranged from £14,000 to £30,000 with the largest proportion of salaries (17.4%) concentrated at just over £21,000. Salary levels in 2007 tended to adjust to the cost of living and most organisations remain cautious stating that they are currently competitive and appropriate for this level. The likelihood for 2009 therefore is that salaries will be dictated by inflation. Interestingly, the website for Prospects Career Services refers to a survey that states students nearing the end of their studies are being realistic about their earning potential. They appear to be conscious of the 'lessening exclusivity of a university degree' and are taking a more pragmatic approach to their anticipated income.

At the moment, basic salaries at entry-level media sales vary quite a bit but, broadly speaking, range between £14,000 and £23,000 with some companies offering basic salaries either side. However, the commissions on sales made will add significantly to the package. If there is a job on offer at around £16,000 to £19,000 basic plus commission and a pay review twice within the year, then this is a good proposition but should still be carefully weighed against other important factors:

- What is the company's reputation in publishing?
- What reputation does the product on which I will be working have within the sector it represents? How established is it in the market?
- How much competition is there and what are the recent advertising revenue trends?
- How are the commission structured and what are the anticipated earnings?
- What is the training provision like in terms of quantity, quality and areas covered?
- What are the promotion prospects?

Getting into a good company that offers excellent training and the opportunity to work on a good product is more important than getting the highest basic salary. I appreciate that university debt creates a dark cloud in one's life and a £20k salary may appear more attractive than one at £16k but, as with buying anything, there has to be more than one consideration.

In terms of salaries further up the scale, salespeople responsible for selling display advertisements can expect to get around £20,000 to £28,000 as a basic. Realistically, you can anticipate this option will be available after about two years at an entry-level position depending on progress. Some folk are able to secure this salary band far quicker while for others it can take longer. In the sales industry, achievement is extremely transparent and success tends to be well rewarded. Currently, Advertisement Managers receive about £35,000 as a basic and Group Advertisement Managers or advertisement directors are on around £45,000 depending on experience and degree of responsibility. The current average salary for publishers is around the £65,000 to £75,000 mark, again reflecting the level of responsibility. Group Publishers' salaries can be over £100k. All these positions are sales-related roles, so there will be some form of bonus or commission on top of the basic wage.

Choosing where to work should not be based on how much the company pays, whether or not you get a company car or fresh flowers on your desk each morning but whether the job is actually right for you and the company is able to offer longer-term career options.

8. Print and online sales

The basic principles of selling are the same everywhere. How they are applied varies, depending on the product being sold, the market and the personality of the salesperson, but the methods remain constant. The differences between selling advertising space online and in print are limited, perhaps, to the variance in language used and the methods of measurement. For print we talk about 'circulation' and 'readership', whereas when we sell online we discuss 'page impressions' and 'unique users'. How the audience is measured is determined by the type of media being discussed. For television, the audience is described in terms of 'ratings', which represent a percentage of a given demographic audience, while radio uses the terms 'reach' and 'impacts'.

The point is that every form of media offers the same solution, which is to access a specific audience. The objective, therefore, is to convince media buyers that our product, be it online, print, TV, mobile integrated advertising, or even the odd poster placed in the public lavatories at motorway services, delivers access to their customers, cost effectively.

When websites as marketing tools first began to appear, there was some concern regarding the impact this would have on more traditional advertising vehicles such as magazines. Bristol-based management communications firm Sift provides the technological support and systems that connect people to information online. They produced some recent research that asked more than 20 UK b2b publishing houses about the impact of online on traditional print-based products. One in three said that online contributes to about 30% of their annual turnover with a significant rise anticipated in the next couple of years. The report concluded that most business publishers were aware of the imminent shift to business information being increasingly accessed online. However, only 16% of those interviewed stated online was likely to replace print, believing that print and online would be used equally.

This investigation complemented research conducted among 300 business decision-makers by the Association of Online Publishers

(AOP) mentioned earlier. Some 39% cited leading search engines such as Google as the most useful resource in their work. A total of 24% of those questioned cited b2b websites as the most useful in accessing sector-specific information, with 14% favouring print. AOP found that 82% of business decision-makers spend an average of one hour each day viewing online sources.

In the same year, a survey conducted by the Periodical Publishers Association (PPA) found that 81% of business decision-makers preferred magazines for providing thorough market coverage with 8% preferring the internet. The survey discovered that 44% of business decision-makers preferred b2b magazines to help them select suppliers compared with only 19% who preferred the internet for this purpose.

So the outcome clearly depends on who and what you ask. However, the UK's online population has now reached 32.5m people with 90% having broadband and this market is worth literally billions of pounds. We may conclude that there is enough to cater for all preferences. In my view, the point is summed up by a quote taken from Hans-Peter Eisinger, global media director at Siemens AG, who recently said:

"We as an advertiser must buy our target audience. You as the media owner, deliver our target audience as your readers and users – you own them."

All media compete with each other and always will, and the media industry will always be interested in how they compare. This quote refocuses the attention on the real issue, which is the target audience. The purpose of advertising in the media is to reach customers and, irrespective of the type of medium, media owners need to prove conclusively that their product reaches more of the right people.

Inevitably if there are separate sales teams for online and print, there will be competition for the largest share of advertising revenue. A magazine sales team may pitch to the same clients as those selling an online product and will obviously try to persuade a client to use one as opposed to the other. A common objection from prospective advertisers is their claim to be spending their advertising budgets on the other!

As the Sift survey earlier revealed, many publishing houses continue to realign their business proposition to accommodate the increasingly dominant online product and are becoming media neutral or even web-centric. Being able to offer access to customers by providing print *and* online products will inevitably mean increased interaction between media owners and their customers, which is never a bad thing, as well as more revenue opportunity for publishers. This only works, however, if the publisher can get the attention of the customers that the advertiser would like to target. Broadly speaking from the advertiser's perspective, it may not matter how he reaches his customers, as long as he does.

In the early years, commercial websites were an unknown quantity in terms of value and heavily linked to established print brands to help sell them to advertisers. In some cases, advertisers were given a 'free trial' to encourage take-up or sold on the back of print advertising to avoid having to negotiate on prices. Nowadays, publishers are able to more accurately measure the impact of online advertising and so the value is far more quantifiable. Publishers are not wasting this opportunity and are investing heavily in website development. Part of their response has been to provide additional sales training for existing sales staff in how to sell more than one media which may include print, online and perhaps sponsorship.

As I mentioned earlier, this is becoming known as Portfolio Selling – *to pitch a proposition that extends across a number of different media*. Needless to say, this requires basic application of exactly the same principles as traditional selling except perhaps with one or two adjustments. Salespeople working on a portfolio of products need to understand the nuances of each product type and be able to speak the language of the media. Quite obviously, salespeople selling digital advertising have to be able to explain the value their product provides with clarity and precision. In order to do this, they need to be aware of the methods of measurement and what is and what is not possible. Publishers are able to accurately report how many users have viewed a page online and indeed how long a page has been viewed. By contrast, it is not possible to tell how many members of the public have actually looked at an advertisement on leather travel bags on page 195 in 'Weekend Escapes' magazine.

Salespeople responsible for selling print and online will need to understand how the various media complement each other as well as the strengths and limitations of each. They should avoid aiming to pitch everything to every client and instead question more to understand and then tailor solutions with greater accuracy. The challenge is to absorb the information quickly and be concise in explanation.

Those wishing to use internet sites to advertise products are generally charged according to the size of the user base. However, we are already seeing a progressive change towards rates being determined by value not size. Websites will have even more detailed personalisation strategies to make the identification of users far more accurate, which makes real-time user recognition achievable. They will be able to target so accurately that it will inevitably increase the overall value of the internet as an advertising option still further. We are at the beginning of the online revolution from a commercial perspective, which can only increase the career opportunities and potential areas in which to specialise for media salespeople entering the business today.

9. The sales department

In publishing, a life in sales usually starts with the role of entry-level media sales executive. A team of executives is usually run by a telesales advertisement manager reporting to a publisher or director. The department consists of a number of other like-minded individuals all with the responsibility of making a number of calls to existing and potentially new advertisers. This department is generally an enjoyable place to be. Co-workers tend to be similar in age and outlook and the manager is often not that much older. The work is hard and sometimes repetitive but can be very lucrative and excellent fun. I should add that with the likelihood of entry-level media sales executives being handed the responsibility of selling both print and online, the role now provides even greater diversity.

In the larger, better-known publishing houses, sales training will be offered in the first few weeks of joining. This is a good area to ask about during an interview and, if the training supplied appears meagre in comparison to others, reconsider the option. The specific training is usually accompanied by a more general welcome to the business through an induction programme, in which you are informed about benefits, expectations, rules, etiquette and so on, to make the early days easier.

On arrival, you will be shown to your seat, introduced to your computer and phone, and if you're very lucky a pen and pad will also be supplied. Gone are the days when we had to try to sell advertising by means of semaphore.

There will be access to a client record system of some type, which will give you the information needed to contact clients. The client data also records any information relating to previous advertising activity. The types of systems used for keeping track of clients vary but usually involve a form of software that allows easy access and plenty of room for comment and general information. The working week will be dominated by telephone sales calls but seasoned with team banter and the odd managerial interruption or team meeting. Product training is also very likely to appear on the agenda, along with introductions to key people around the building. I always used to welcome new members with a lunch or an evening pint but, either way, there will be plenty of opportunity for you to get to know your new workmates. The employer or manager will be keen to ensure that your first few weeks are as comfortable and welcoming as possible, so if you are uncertain about anything, please do not hesitate to ask someone.

One of the toughest challenges in the early days of a sales job is making the first call. Everyone around you appears to stop what they are doing and listen. Well, even if they do, so what? No one deliberately fails first time. Everyone has to learn and learning is about practising, which involves mistakes. I remember my first day at one company in London. I had decided to drive but failed to anticipate the traffic, which switched from crawl to total gridlock. I was late on my very first day and mortified to demonstrate my total ineptitude at being able to turn up on time. The manager was very kind actually. He was probably in shock that anyone could manage to be late on their first day. I know I was. The point is that people forgive mistakes when you're learning; it is mistakes when you are supposed to know what you are doing that cause the biggest problems. So when that moment comes – relax by thinking that this is one of the few moments in life when you will be forgiven for getting something wrong.

As I have mentioned, the primary activity of the sales team is making telephone calls. The number of calls will vary according to the product but on a weekly it is likely you will make between 50 and 120 calls a day. This may seem a lot but the bottom line is the more calls you make the more you will sell. As I mentioned in the introduction, the calls themselves don't take very long so it is entirely possible to make 120 calls in one day and get all the requisite administration done as well.

When I said calls equal sales a moment ago, I feel I should qualify that a little. My view is that lots of calls do indeed mean greater volume of sales. However, slightly fewer but better quality calls will maximise effectiveness and increase revenues still further. As they say, being busy doesn't mean you're being effective. I would say that the majority of those who work late in their jobs wouldn't need to if they knew how to a) delegate or b) manage their time.

Everything takes more time at first. As we learn, we become better and things take less time to complete. We have a sense of control and satisfaction about our work. As our proficiency develops, others expect and ask more of us and our time begins to become stretched once again. At this point we need to begin *planning* and scheduling our work which is a skill in its own right. We need to develop the ability to discern between the important and the urgent and allocate enough time in our diaries to get everything done to a satisfactory standard. I tend to think of time being similar to money in that there is only so much of it and once spent, it's gone. Imagine instead of someone asking for an hour of your time, they asked you for £30 in cash. Not many would be willing to hand over this amount of money and the reason is quite simply that you need it. It's the same with time, once handed over, you no longer have it and whatever you needed to do with that time doesn't get done. I'm not saying be mean to other people but I am saying treat your time with respect as you would your income. There is only a finite amount of it available.

Selling advertising space is about being efficient with time as there is a lot of additional activity not directly related to sales. Below is a list of a few other activities associated with selling media advertising space.

Call logging

Most managers will use the volume of calls made by staff as one measure of departmental and individual effectiveness. Salespeople, therefore, are required to complete a call log sheet detailing who they called and whether or not it was an 'effective call'. An effective call is defined as being one in which the salesperson gets through to the individual responsible for buying advertising space and explains the product benefits. In some cases, installed phone systems are able to record outgoing and incoming call volumes, by extension. This means on request to the administration or IT department, the sales manager can access the required information without having to get the salespeople to complete a form.

Production record 'book'

All types of products in publishing houses will have cut-off points when the selling period ends. Unsurprisingly to some perhaps, a weekly magazine will have a weekly deadline. This means on the pre-agreed day, all the advertisement space is filled and the editorial is written. The next stage is for the magazine to be put together by the production staff so it is ready to be printed. The various sections of the magazine that contain advertising may have different deadlines and so may 'close' at different times. For online products, there is no printing required and advertising and editorial is entered onto the website as it becomes available. This means there are no actual deadlines to reach, although managers may impose deadlines to encourage effort and create a sense of completion for those working in this medium.

Lead sourcing

It may seem obvious but any sole trader, small business or blue-chip corporation that might conceivably want to advertise should be contacted by the relevant sales force. Potential advertisers are called 'leads' and are sourced from anywhere! 'Anywhere' stretches from press information received in the mail, to conversation with others in the industry and looking through the pages of competing magazines.

Competitor analysis

'Competitors' include any product in any medium that is capable of taking away advertising revenue from your product. Analysing the competition means we will know who is advertising, how often and what size of advertisements they are buying and roughly what proportion of revenue we get as opposed to others in this sector. Usually the advertisement manager will organise competitor analysis within the team although sometimes this information is generated by others and supplied to the relevant sales departments.

Sales recording

The methods and systems used to support sales activity vary enormously. Some departments still use a 'Production Book', which is a hard copy method of ensuring sales are recorded. The records include advertisement sizes, length of run (every week or month etc), the salesperson responsible, the client, the date booked and the price paid. Additional details can be added, such as where in the section the advertisement is to appear (if there has been a request) or if the advertisement is new or to be repeated, or taken from another publication. Salespeople may also have to record this information on a computer network so related departments such as accounts and production are informed. It is generally true that as sales are made, they are entered into the system or onto a spreadsheet, to avoid mistakes. This function then becomes part of the working day for salespeople.

Post, fax and email

Along with the excitement and the challenge of the job come the more mundane tasks. In my day, we used to have to set aside an hour a day to put together the media information and stuff it in an envelope. However, now we've emerged from the Victorian age, all this can be done by email, which is a lot quicker. Fax machines are seldom used these days and have virtually drifted into history books along with vinyl records, VHS cassettes and the majority of my suits. The point here is less to do with how sales and selling is administered and more to do with how you control it. Dealing with large numbers of emails can very easily eat into prime selling time. The main function of the job is to call prospective advertisers and all other activity, with the possible exception of going to the toilet, is less important. (Although I have heard of a case where a draconian manager actually restricted toilet visits to three times a day!) Administrative duties such as post, fax and email should wait until there is a lull in the working day. Usually, managers like their sales staff to undertake administration around lunchtime or after five o'clock. These are times when it is less easy to get hold of prospective advertisers and should be used for less frontline activity.

Attend internal meetings

It is true that to some people having a meeting means sitting in a comfortable chair, sipping coffee from a porcelain mug and munching on a biscuit. While it's a lovely way to get paid, it is also true that poorly planned internal meetings absorb a lot of the working day and contribute less to it than any other known office activity apart from not actually turning up for work.

Ad hoc communication during the working day is inevitable and in some cases beneficial but it has to be under control. I see a good many office folk who are keen on holding spontaneous meetings to share information. In my experience, this type of meeting has only one effect, which is to guarantee that work will stop flowing. Unless lives are at risk or, worse, there is a chance of losing money, unplanned meetings or lengthy discussions are not recommended. All staff should choose an appropriate time to communicate issues or ask questions in order to decrease interruptions. The media sales job requires concentration and lots of effort so a continuous stream of questions between people will inevitably disrupt. It is likely you will attend meetings to discuss progress, problems, targets and strategy during the week on perhaps one or two occasions. Prior to any meeting, you should be informed what it's about, how long it will take, when and where it will take place and you should receive an agenda or at the very least an email highlighting the key areas for discussion. If you do want to discuss things with your manager, ask yourself whether or not it can wait till the scheduled meeting and, if not, choose a time when the manager is likely to be able to devote enough time to help you.

Managing your time as an entry-level media salesperson is crucial to the role. Office administration and internal meetings or ad hoc and lengthy conversations can eat time in huge quantities.

Liaising with other staff

Obviously you will have to liaise with other people involved with the process of creating a media product. Your main circle of communication is detailed below.

FAR ENVIRONMENT
Accounts Dept.
Publishing Director
Human Resources

NEAR ENVIRONMENT
Adv. Production Dept.
Publisher
Editorial Dept.
Training Dept.

IMMEDIATE ENVIRONMENT
Advertisement Manager
Other Classified Sales
Executives on team

Media sales executive – internal contact environments (likely to vary according to which type of company you join)

Daily communication lines are with your team and manager. Communication will also extend to the publisher and production department. It will also include discussing the occasional accounts query with the credit control department. Accounts queries usually refer to clients that have a bill outstanding or are known to be poor payers. It's very important to get along with your fellow salespeople and editorial colleagues. Being a team player is an important competency (refer to KPIs for explanation) in the media sales role and means just that – to work co-operatively with others, to be part of a team, to work together and to make an effort to be sensitive to the needs of other people. The amount of time spent on each area obviously depends on the exact nature of the role.

Teamworking and effective communication are, of course, not exclusive to media sales roles. The requirement not to engage with other people is only required if you have been selected to manage a single occupancy space station somewhere in the Delta Minor region of Xenoth, or have been given a small business loan to open an internet café in the Sangre de Cristo mountain range.

10. Typical clients

The types of clients a media salesperson might contact at entry level will vary depending on the sector and type of magazine but, broadly speaking, these are the main categories of clients that a media sales executive should anticipate talking to.

- **Clients** who are buying advertisement space for themselves as sole trader, or working for a larger company. They are usually providing a service or product range that will appeal to the readership or user-base. Decisions on whether to buy advertisement space are relatively quick as the responsibility only falls to one person.

- **Agencies** or consultancies working on behalf of a single client or number of client companies. Agencies are responsible for the creative output, the media planning and buying. Decisions can take a bit longer as they can involve more than one person but in general the better the relationship, the more likely they are to buy.

For print or online business to business products, entry-level media sales executives will find themselves responsible for selling recruitment advertisement space (job ads). They will be speaking to one of three types of individual:

- **Clients direct** – professionals (perhaps in Human Resources, or the department head) looking to advertise a position on behalf of their company.

- **Agencies** that have been contracted to provide an advertising campaign by a client company.

- **Recruitment consultancies** that have been hired by a company to provide a full recruitment service on behalf of a client company.

In b2b, the recruitment (job ads) section generates a large proportion of advertising revenue. In some cases, it is the largest contributor. This is true of online b2b products as much as printed magazines. The advertisements appearing here are for jobs related to the industry the published product serves and include a wide range of jobs from board positions to junior assistants. The more jobs are advertised, the more likely the section is to be read by job seekers, which means greater return for both the advertiser and the publishing company.

The advertisements are either placed directly by the company looking to fill a position, or by a company acting on their behalf. These companies are either recruitment agencies or consultancies. An agency is employed by a company looking to fill one or more vacancies. Their responsibilities include receiving the remit from the client for the post or posts they wish to fill, creating a suitable advertisement and contacting the publishing houses to negotiate advertisement rates. An agency buys the space but anyone wishing to apply for the position should apply directly to the recruiting client and not the agency.

There are a number of different types of advertising agency in existence. Depending on size they will offer a range of services from media buying only to full service, which includes media planning, creating the advertisements and buying the media space. Over the last few years, we have seen companies emerging that are digital buying shops or companies that specialise in buying online advertisement space on behalf of clients. These companies are able to plan and buy space for clients and measure the impact of the advertising.

Some larger agencies also have a specific recruitment department. Agencies charge their clients for the service they provide and also receive a 10-15% discount from publishers on all advertising placed due to the volume of business they provide. The only area agencies are not involved with is the candidate selection process.

A recruitment consultancy, like an agency, works on behalf of a client, but their expertise extends to the interview and selection process and is not restricted to media planning and buying. A consultancy places the advertising where they believe they will get the best response and requests that the applicants reply directly to them. They act as a bridge between the applicant and the recruiting company to help with the legwork associated with the recruitment process, adding a good deal of selection and interview experience and skill. A consultancy may be employed if there are a number of vacancies available at one company and internal resources cannot be devoted to a lengthy recruitment process. Clients using a consultancy do not want applicants to apply directly for any number or reasons. It may be they do not have the internal resource to handle the number of likely applicants, or the skill and experience required to make an appropriate decision. It may be that the position they seek to fill is sensitive and has to be handled with discretion. It is for these reasons that the recruiting company is not mentioned in the advertisements. Whatever the reason, a consultancy is an extremely useful external resource and is very often used for business appointments.

Like agencies, consultancies are interested in cultivating excellent working relationships with both their clients and media owners. ('Media owner' is a generic description meaning companies that literally own the type of media used.)

The third type of advertiser seen to be placing advertising in the recruitment section of a b2b product is the client direct. Not all clients use agencies or consultancies to help them seek the right individual. Some prefer to run their own recruitment programme, handling all the stages themselves. The reasons they may choose to go it alone will vary from lack of funds for commissioning an external company to the likelihood that the recruitment process will be relatively straightforward.

It is very important for entry-level media sales personnel responsible for selling recruitment advertisement space to forge relationships with these key clients as they represent the largest prospective revenue to any weekly b2b magazine. I say weekly for two reasons. First, recruitment advertisements usually generate quite a good response (depending on the job on offer and the magazine in which the advertisement is placed of course) so there is no real need to continue advertising week in, week out. Continuing to run a job advertisement more than a couple of weeks might well be considered a negative statement about the desirability of the job itself. If a job advertisement lingers in the business press, the target audience may begin to wonder why the recruiting company is having difficulty filling the position. This applies just as much to advertisements selling a house or a car; if it continues to be advertised, people start to believe there must be something wrong with it.

The second reason is that there is a business imperative to re-employ should someone leave. The sooner the position is filled, the less impact it will have on productivity. Weekly publications are obviously published more frequently so the time between having a vacancy and being able to advertise for replacements is minimal. Indeed the attractiveness of online recruitment advertising is even greater due to the fact that a recruiting company can begin advertising within a few hours of agreeing a deal with a media owner as websites are not restricted by print deadlines. I should add that there are perfectly good reasons why recruitment companies might choose to use monthlies or bi-monthlies to advertise their positions. As with all recruitment advertising, the frequency of the exposure matters less than the relevance of the position to the readership.

The size of company will determine how often vacancies emerge and, in general, there are fewer bookings taken by direct clients than recruitment consultancies and agencies. Nonetheless, recruitment salespeople should place high value on these customers. In some cases, due to the low volume of advertisements placed by the individual companies, there is no or little negotiation on price. This means the page yield (average revenue per page) is generally higher, the more direct bookings are taken. So when you are considering working for a b2b magazine or website in the recruitment section, a good sign is that the existing advertising pages are a mix of high-profile recruitment consultancies and agencies and direct clients advertising a range of jobs directly relevant to the sector represented by the magazine or product.

You don't need to grasp all this before you apply for a position in media sales. I might also add that there are some very successful salespeople who never fully analyse the situation in as much detail as I have and just get on with the job.

There are other areas beyond recruitment that also fall into the parameters of entry-level media sales. For a b2b publisher, you may find yourself selling a section called Marketplace, Directory, Index Suppliers or Update. In consumer publishing you may be given a specific category or market to focus on such as Health & Beauty,

Legal or Education. Whatever they are called, all of them provide advertisements for products, services, ideas or named contacts to help the reader.

In most cases, a media salesperson would contact the business direct as opposed to going through an advertising agency, which means working to build relationships with prospective advertisers. Most advertisements in these sections are designed to generate response from prospective customers, but response is only part of the goal. It is also important for advertisers to create company or product recognition within their customer community because, when a customer finally is in a position to buy, he will probably go with the company most familiar to him. One of the problems faced by entry-level media salespeople is that advertising clients tend to measure the effectiveness of their advertisements purely by the volume of response they generate and, when nothing happens, it is usually the magazine that is blamed (see Objection Handling). In life, however, it is the familiar brands that get the business while those new to the market struggle to get a share of sales.

A London shop advertising itself evocatively as a purveyor of musical scores appropriate for the era which in this case was late Edwardian. Broome's traded in Holborn between 1901 and 1914 catering for the home entertainment business which at that point was largely made up of singing around the piano. Songs were mainly of the parlour variety and popular hymns.

Part 4

Mastering the skills

"Wise men speak because they have something to say; Fools because they have to say something."

Plato

11. Greeting the keeper

In media sales, a large proportion of calls targeting individuals responsible for buying media space are fielded by secretaries, PAs or receptionists. These people are commonly called 'gatekeepers'. Metaphorically speaking, they stand at the gate not letting in anyone who is undeserving. Lots of media salespeople, from the raw recruit to the highly skilled, have difficulty getting around this problem person. As we know, however, even the wildest of animals can be tamed, perhaps become friendly or even.....helpful.

Once the phone is answered, you ask the receptionist to put you through to the person in charge of buying advertising space for their company. They may respond by asking about the purpose of your call. You will explain the reason politely and clearly, which in turn usually generates a comment to the effect that they are 'not interested'.

This response is as a result of receiving a high proportion of calls from salespeople during the week and having become conditioned to fobbing them off, on behalf of the boss.

The difficulty is converting them from Rottweiler to helpful friend. Bear in mind they are told to field sales calls but don't have the authority to decide what media to buy, so persistence is called for. It is important to remember that these people can be very influential. Many a hot prospect has cooled due to a negative fly-away comment from gatekeeper to boss. Information that has been sent to a decision-maker may or may not reach them depending on the relationship one has developed with the gatekeeper. So these people are important even though they do not have the authority to decide whether your product is a good marketing choice or not.

In the book *Guerrilla Negotiating* by Levinson Smith & Wilson, the authors talk about how truly effective telesales people gain an advantage by treating gatekeepers with deference and respect. They approach the gatekeeper as if they run the company and get them onside, as it were. Along this theme, I have compiled various techniques from colleagues and personal experience that can be employed.

Little boy lost

"I've just joined XYZ Company and have been told to call and speak to Mr Jones in Marketing. Can you help me please?"

Intended to appeal to the softer, sympathetic side of someone.

Member of the family

"Hello my name is Terry from XYZ Company. Is that (first name of gatekeeper)...? It is? Oh, I'm glad it's you, I was told that you were the best person to speak to about..."

Using flattery as the first line of attack.

Mr Unusual

"Hello can I speak to Claire Smith please?"

"Who is it?"

"My name is Terry from XYZ Company."

"I'm sorry, she's very busy at the moment."

"Oh ok, thanks... (pause)... You probably get lots of these calls don't you?"

"Quite a few, yes."

"I read something interesting the other day. Did you know that in the UK, the average time spent concentrating on one thing at work is down to four minutes? The biggest interruption being phone calls."

"Really?"

"Apparently, yes. Terrible isn't it? And you're right in the middle of it! I don't know how you manage to get anything done!"

"It is difficult, actually."

"You know I'll have to call again, don't you? So when are you least busy during the day, so I don't disrupt things too much?"

None of these come with guarantees but all will help tame the beast.

In the book *Selling by Phone*, the author, Linda Richardson, includes an excellent chapter on handling gatekeepers. She says that ignoring their internal power can be an expensive mistake. She stresses the importance of cultivating and winning the support of the gatekeeper. If you can find a way to help them, they will help you.

Additional tips

- When you do get through to your customer, say supportive things about the gatekeeper – it *will* get back to them.
- Make them feel important.
- Be sensitive – ask them how they are – try to appreciate they are only doing what they are told and that very few people actually enjoy being rude or rebuffing others all day long.
- Ask for their ideas, views and opinions.
- Be interested in *them.*
- Thank them and use their names.
- Building a relationship with them is an investment in the deal you intend to do.
- Show respect, sincerity and be polite.
- Tell the truth and be persistent but not obnoxious.
- Insinuate they work *with* the boss and not *for* the boss.

One last idea

When the gatekeeper says the boss is busy, shriek with pain and laughter and say that you had a run of luck and have got through to the last two clients without a problem and there was a bet in the office that you couldn't make it a hat-trick! Ask if there's any way at all the gatekeeper could save you a fiver.

Another interesting piece of information I read recently is that if the last word you say on a voicemail message to your contact is their first name, the chances of them calling you back can be increased by 25%.

12. A structured approach

Selling, like most tasks, is achieved by applying some fairly straightforward rules. With sales, in order to provide an appropriate solution, one first has to understand the problem. For example, I am not going to buy a pair of yellow trousers if I want a blue pair. The first step in the selling process, therefore, is to ask the right questions to establish the requirements. You need to get to the point where you know what colour trousers, metaphorically, they are looking for.

First, we have to establish the fact that the client is worthy of a call and, having fought your way through the receptionist, the first step is to introduce yourself.

"Hello, my name is Terry Thompson from Rural Retreats magazine."

In the majority of cases the normal courtesies will then take place. In some cases all you will receive is a grunt of stressed disappointment from the client but whatever the response, persevere! The next step is to explain why you're calling.

"The purpose of my call is to discuss your advertising plans for the next few months."

Or, alternatively:

"The purpose of my call is to find out more about your current marketing needs."

The essence is to ensure the client is clear about why you are calling. The next problem to overcome is to reassure the client that you will not take up too much of their time.

"The call won't take more than a few minutes."

You may notice that you are not asking for a few minutes of their time, which gives them an opportunity to say they are too busy. Instead, you are making a statement of intent, which is far more assertive and leaves little room for a negative response. Of course the reality is that we hope it will be a long and prosperous call ending in a huge order enabling you to retire to the country and live off the commission for the rest of your life. However, to get their attention and to reassure them you are sensitive to how busy they are, we mention that the call will be short. Even in a minute or so, it is amazing how much information you can find out from clients – and any length of communication allows us to begin building rapport. Once we have got into the call, we can begin the process of asking questions to find out what their needs are.

Questions are the lifeblood of any sales conversation. Without the right information there is little chance of providing an attractive solution. There are two basic types of questions: *open* and *closed*.

An open question ensures the recipient has to answer relatively fully. They begin with one of the following:

- Who....
- What....
- Where....
- How....
- Why....
- When....

Asking a question using one of the above will ensure information is gathered quickly. Although one interesting observation is that the only truly open question begins with 'Why'. This is because all the others gather facts while 'Why' extracts an opinion or reason. Asking someone's opinion on something suggests interest in them and contributes to creating a good platform for rapport. However, care should be taken as the 'why' question can also be misinterpreted. *"Why did you choose to advertise in Country Places Magazine?"* or *"Why didn't you use us?"* might be interpreted as a challenge to their choice and invoke a defensive reaction. Therefore, in selling, question structure is very important. Prefacing questions that might be considered difficult or contentious is one way to soften the approach. An example would be to preface the first question by saying, *"It would be helpful to know why you chose to advertise in Y publication."* Even better would to rephrase the question entirely by asking, *"What makes you choose one product over another?"* The preface prepares the recipient for what may be considered a moderately invasive question and lowers the risk of sounding impertinent.

Another area I always believe worth investigating is the subject of budget. Asking how much money a client has can be useful when planning a pitch. If we have little idea of what the budget might be, then our proposal may be way too high or way too low. However, if we were to ask *"How much money have you got?"* it will probably create a negative reaction particularly early in the call. Salespeople have to earn the right to ask these types of questions, developing the relationship by building trust and respect. Once the trust is there, asking about budget or, preferably, the *investment* level will be acceptable. Once the relationship has reached this stage, not only are we able to probe deeper but our suggestions and advice on marketing or advertising will be well received. One crucial thing to remember is that in media sales, we should aim to create a conversational selling approach and not interrogate the client. We need to extract the right information but in a conversational way.

While I'm on the matter of conversation, it is worth observing that the subject matter we enjoy speaking about most is ourselves. We know all there is to know (or at least we think we do) about this subject and of course it's fascinating in every way. We give our opinions, our knowledge and our experience in conversation because it challenges us least and appears to us to be of interest and relevance to the interaction. We like it when we are asked our opinion because it makes us feel valued and we react well when someone appears interested in what we say. Thus interaction between people can easily support that basic human need for self-esteem. Conversation that is based around 'self' tends to be anecdotal in its nature. For example:

A: *"Are you going out this weekend?"*
B: *"Yes, I'm going shopping in Bluewater."*
A: *"Really? That'll be good. I went shopping last weekend to buy a new watch."*

B: *"Oh, have you seen mine? It's a Rolex! It's a fake! Good though isn't it?!"*
A: *"Yeah. It's great. I bought a fake watch in Thailand. It was so cheap but then I got it wet and it never worked again!"*
B: *"Thailand? I went there. I love the food and the people are so friendly and we visited the islands and just chilled out."*
A: *"That's what I do on holidays...."*

This interaction starts nicely with an enquiring question from A to B. Then it shifts so that each time A or B says something it is about *their* experience based on chosen information taken from previous comment. At no point after the first question is there any enquiry from A or B about the other. One might ask if A and B really care about each other at all. Perhaps A could have made an effort to ask B more about the trip to Bluewater and perhaps B could have shown a little more interest in the fake Rolex.

I hear this type of conversation quite a bit and decided to test my theory out on a colleague. My strategy was to not offer any view or opinion of my own, recount any story or personal experience unless requested to do so by the other person. In other words, I was going to ask them about them, until they decided to ask about me.

I did find it difficult *not* talking about me, which in a way proves the point that self-focused conversation tends to dominate and that what we hear we relate to our own experience and knowledge. At about 7.30pm I started the conversation with something like *"So! How's the job?"* and continued with things like *"How did you do that?"* and *"Oh no! What did you do then?"* seasoning the interaction with plenty of encouragement along the way. I had to wait until a little before 10pm for them to ask about something in my life. This may prove I surround myself with egotists or that I have reached un-chartered heights of cynicism or that apparent 'good' conversation centres around self-interest.

Some people engaging in this type of anecdotal conversation almost appear to vie or compete for airspace in order to reiterate a funny story, sad experience or personal opinion related to them. However, truly good conversation has to be tempered with genuine interest in others.

A better quality conversation might be as follows:

A: *"What are you doing this weekend?"*
B: *"I'm going to shopping in Bluewater."*
A: *"Really. Why Bluewater particularly?"*
B: *"It's just a massive mall with loads of choice and you don't get wet if it rains. Have you been?"*
A: *"No but I've heard it's great."*
B: *"Where do you go shopping?"*
A: *"Oh locally, mainly. But I love going up to Oxford Street to window shop. Do you ever get up there?"*
B: *"Only once. I can't stand the crowds. What's it like these days?"*

This interaction is more balanced. It helps that both individuals are prepared to sacrifice some 'me' time in order to let someone else have a go. Of course, this is a far more satisfying interaction and could establish whether there is synergy between personality types and whether or not a friendship could grow.

Although not really linked to telephone sales, another interesting and common trait is for people's loss of interest in conversation to be reflected in their non-verbal behaviour, when the subject switches to someone else. Typical signs are that there is a loss of eye contact or perhaps their eyes, although heading in our general direction, become glazed and a non-expressive facial stare emerges. Their facial reactions suggest we are failing to entertain them sufficiently, mainly because the conversation doesn't directly involve or include them. They may also become distracted, perhaps occasionally glancing around in their immediate environment for something more interesting, or commonly have a quick check for messages on their mobile at the same time as 'listening' to the other person. This behaviour is not deliberate or even conscious but it does demonstrate a lack of emotional intelligence as to the needs of others in conversation. It doesn't necessitate a change of friends but confirms the immutable fact of life that we are all interested in ourselves.

The reason I mention this is not to demonstrate how age increases cynicism but to show how to create or build rapport. Being interested in someone else flatters that individual and it gives them the opportunity to tell you about themselves. We listen, enquire and give them the impression that what they are doing is important, interesting, clever, inspired or perhaps unusual. Questions are without doubt the lifeblood of any conversation. Avoid asking one question after another with a mere grunt of acceptance punctuating the given answers and try to listen properly to what someone is saying to give you the direction of the conversation.

The first part of the second example demonstrates this nicely. Person A has picked something from the answer to their previous question in order to follow on. Thus there is continuity and flow.

A: *"Are you going out this weekend?"*
B: *"Yes, I'm going to shopping in Bluewater."*
A: *"Really? Why Bluewater particularly?"*

An effective conversation in a sales context may consist of this:

Seller : *"I hear you're in the middle of a merger at the moment."*
Buyer: *"Yes and it's hell. So much happening to the product range and we're moving offices."*
Seller: *"That does sound a bit much. Where are you moving to?"*
Buyer: *"Bristol. It's a long way but nearer to the factory."*
Seller: *"Does being in Bristol mean you can keep an eye on production?"*

While this conversation hasn't brought any information that could help make a sale as yet, it has developed the relationship. The seller has used their knowledge of the company to open the conversation, empathy to the usual difficulties associated with mergers, acknowledgement of the new location and possible implications. This means that work has begun to develop the trust and respect needed as the foundation to effective sales.

You may also notice that there aren't many open questions here. There is only one in fact, in the fourth line. While many sales training programmes state that open questions are the working tools of a salesperson it is also true that they form only part of a typical conversation. If our goal is to have a fact-finding, rapport-building conversation then we should consider the value of both open and closed questions. The term 'closed questions' implies they close down communication, but this is not always true. They can help us achieve agreement and 'buy-in' to the salesperson's point and therefore help to construct an effective sales call. While open questions help extract a broader explanation of the client's situation, closed questions form another important part of conversation structure and reflect a more realistic type of interaction.

Questions help us extract the most relevant information and we should aim to base all sales question on the **BOM** model, which guides us as to the subjects we should aim to cover.

> **B**ackground
> **O**bjective
> **M**ethod

Broadly speaking, this is finding out *who* they are (**B**), *what* they want to achieve (**O**) and *how* they are going to achieve it (**M**).

In the context of entry-level media sales this might involve the following question areas.

Background
- What does this company do?
- What products do they have?
- Where are they based?
- What size is this company?

Objective
- What are their advertising objectives?
- Who are they trying to reach (target audience)?
- What are the key messages being sent by the advertising?
- How will they monitor progress?

Method
- How are they doing?
- **Who is responsible for making decisions on where to advertise?**
- What have they done in the past?
- What are they doing currently?

- What are their plans for future marketing or advertising?
- What is their level of investment for the coming months/year?

Clearly not all these questions are appropriate to ask everyone on every call and in some cases the type of question would alter depending on what section within the magazine is being sold. For example if you were selling recruitment advertising, the questions may have to be adjusted or changed. Using the BOM model, questions related to the recruitment sale may be as follows.

Background
- How often do they appear to recruit?
- What sort of vacancies have come up?
- **Who is responsible buying advertising?**
- What size company are they?
- Are they looking for staff at the moment?

Objective
- What type of people do they want to reach?
- How quickly do they need to fill the role?
- **How close are they to making decisions?**
- What are their criteria for choosing a magazine in which to advertise?
- Is it important to brand the company as well as advertise the job?

Method
- How have they recruited in the past?
- Which methods do they find most effective?
- **How are advertising decisions made?**
- **Who is involved with making advertising decisions?**
- What plans do they have in place already?
- What is their level of investment?

These form the basis of the type of information that we need in order to build the sale.

Working out what we need to know is relatively straightforward and is captured in the above question model. If I were to limit myself, which is difficult enough in itself, I would try and extract the following information as a minimum.

- Who are their customers (or candidates if it's a recruitment call)? Are they recruiting?
- What are their advertising/marketing objectives?
- **Who makes decisions on advertising spend?**
- Timeframes for marketing or advertising.
- Any additional criteria on which they decide where to advertise.

The 'criteria' question is a good one. It does a couple of important things during a conversation. First, it helps to take the focus away from a price and secondly, the response is usually a list of things that the buyer needs to see are on offer, before he will say yes.

As an example, answer these questions:

1. What were your criteria before you moved to where you are living now?
2. What are your criteria for a good friend?
3. What would your criteria be if you wanted a better job?

You probably found yourself building a list in your mind in order to offer a reply. All the above questions extract what are commonly termed 'needs'. These define the client's advertising or marketing goals.

There are other important areas to investigate besides needs-based questions and these are highlighted in bold type above.

They are called 'decisional questions'. These highlight the plausibility of getting deals agreed. Question areas such as who makes decisions on placing advertising, what the process to getting decisions might be and how long decisions usually take will ensure we have all the facts.

From time to time, the sales manager will want to know what the sales prospects are from each member of the team. A 'sales prospect' is defined as a sale that is near to conclusion and is most likely be booked by the client before the next sales deadline. This information helps the manager work out where the revenue figure may end up against the target for that sales period. Sales executives are expected to provide a list of prospects that are at this stage in the sale. Decisional questions help executives with this information. One method of defining them works as follows:

A

If a client is keen to place advertising as soon as possible and is able to make the decision themselves, this prospect can be classified as an 'A' lead (**i.e. likely and imminent**).

B

If a client is keen to place advertising but has to put the option to the board for a decision, which usually takes a couple of weeks, then this prospect can be classified as 'B' prospect (**i.e. likely but not imminent**).

C

If a client has expressed an interest but is not in a position to place an order due to a delay in the decision-making process (perhaps there are others that have to be involved with the decision) this prospect can be classified as 'C' prospect (**i.e. possible but not for a while**).

It is important for a sales executive to keep track of sales progress in order to be able to provide the manager with the correct information when it is required as well as to ensure they are spending their time working on the clients that are most likely to buy.

Overall, effective questioning will allow us to understand the following:

* Who the client is.
* What they need to achieve.
* When they want to promote.

- What we have to prove about our product to convince them.
- How decisions are made and who is involved with the decision process.
- How and where we may be able to help.

There is one other type of question that helps to glue the early part of the sales process together even more successfully. This takes the form of linked questions.

Linked questions permit us to gain agreement from the client to an 'ideal' situation before we begin speaking about our product features and benefits.

For example, if I sell advertising space in a marketing magazine I may ask:

"Presumably to save money, you want to reach only senior marketing personnel with authority to spend budget?"

The answer will inevitably be "yes", in which case we can solve the problem because this is the audience that reads our magazine.

Another (related to recruitment advertising sales):

"I'm assuming you want to advertise quickly in order to ensure you fill your vacancy as soon as possible?"

The reply will inevitably be affirmative again, as an empty seat at any organisation clearly costs the business money.

The point is that both these questions ask the client to confirm they seek a solution that we know we can provide. The only difference is that we haven't yet explained that our product or service can actually provide it.

Once we have built rapport and understood or discussed the needs with a customer, we can then take it to the next stage.

To round off the questioning or probing aspect to the sale, we *summarise*. Summarising the salient points in a sale accomplishes a number of things. It clarifies the needs, focuses the call on the most important aspects and also checks we have understood everything correctly. The client at this stage will listen to your summary and hopefully agree that these are indeed his primary requirements. A summary should be short and clear. It should include all the needs you aim to fulfil in the next part of the sale. It may also be a wise move to ask a final question to see if there is anything else that might be worth considering before moving on. An example is as follows.

Salesperson: *"To sum up then, Pete, you have a vacancy for a web developer at your company. You need to fill this position as quickly as possible but with the right type of person. Naturally, you want to spend the least amount of money but reach as many potential candidates as possible. The advertisement also needs to strengthen your company's brand and be designed to attract quality people. Is that about it?"*

Pete (the client):   *"Yes, that sounds right."*

Salesperson: *"Is there anything else we should consider before we move on?"*

Pete: *"Well, perhaps I should mention we have a new company logo that has to appear in all marketing literature from this month. It's not ready for another two weeks though."*

The final 'checking' question from the salesperson has established something that didn't emerge at the initial probing stage but has relevance to this sale. Changing a logo has implications for a company's market recognition and, if it is changed, should be promoted as much as possible. As a result of this information, it would be relevant to suggest additional advertising with the aim of ensuring the new logo becomes recognisable within the market quickly. The other issue that has emerged is that the new logo won't be ready for two weeks. This has implications for closing the deal. Maybe he will not be able to place any advertising until the logo is available. Whatever the situation, at least you are aware of it and can adjust the solution you offer accordingly.

Probing or questioning allows us to understand more about how and where we may be able to help clients. The summary recaps the key client 'needs' and the 'checking question' helps to capture any additional information that may be used during the sale. More on this later.

I should perhaps reiterate the point that, with the exception of call centres and telemarketing operations, this type of sales call is rarely scripted. This means that publishing companies entrust individuals to be able to think on their feet, use a logical and reasonable approach to dealing with customers and take decisions about how far to go and what to ask. This means that very few calls will permit you to ask all the questions covered so far. We have to use our own personal judgement as to what will make the call succeed. Too many questions may seem intrusive and interrogational, while too few will prevent us from achieving our sales goals.

13. Our products – and how to make them sound excellent

As I have mentioned, it is crucial in sales to know as much as possible about the product we are selling, the industry or sector it relates to and the competition.

If we do, then it is likely we could talk about our product for several days, pausing only to eat an occasional chocolate muffin. While the muffin remains clear of blame, salespeople fall into the trap of drowning clients with too much 'product talk'. As I have mentioned, we tend to talk about things that interest us and things we know a good deal about. However, it is also true that a great many people spend hours talking about things they know very little about. Many of us can claim to have a made a living out of it but when selling, we have to be able to discern the relevant from the irrelevant when discussing our products. Of course, there are plenty of people out there in any walk of life who fail to distinguish between the relevant and the irrelevant. It might be argued that as a result of global shrinkage and general information overload, the irrelevant has infiltrated most aspects of existence. Irrespective of this, salespeople have to remember that the objective is to make a sale and not give a monologue.

Despite the requirement of a media salesperson to make lots of calls every day, it is equally important to treat each call as unique and not consider the job repetitive. Some people ask me how I can deliver the same sales courses again and again without becoming bored or losing enthusiasm. My answer is simply that as a result of trainer/delegate interaction, the points raised, the group dynamic, differing delegate skill and experience levels, every day has a unique make-up. The only job that never changes and could be termed repetitive and unchanging is one without human interaction. There are few jobs designed without some form of contact because our species needs communication. Even factories where nothing can be heard for hours on end apart from machinery will have social clubs or canteens where individuals can interact.

The answer is that every hour is unique and brings a slightly different experience, which helps us understand why making 80 calls a day every day for 48 working weeks a year is acceptable and even enjoyable. As I mentioned in an earlier chapter, calling is not the entire job anyway, and there are many other areas to the job of media sales.

In a sales context, we have to ensure that the questions we ask, what we say about our product and even the language we use vary in accordance with what is relevant. If a client is interested only in reaching marketing managers at a cost-effective price, then there is little relevance to banging on about the fact that the magazine has 16 pages of news featured every week. Choose what you say about the magazine in accordance with the interests or needs of the customer to whom you are speaking at that moment. The way to do this is to develop a repertoire of features and benefits and then, depending on the client's needs, choose which ones are relevant.

A *feature* is defined as something that is factual about a product. It has to be indisputable and not based on opinion or hearsay.

The *benefit* explains what the client will receive as a consequence of the product having that specific quality or feature.

An example:

- A **feature** of a telephone is that is has speed-dial.
- The **benefit** is that it saves you time when you have to make a call.

Another:

- A **feature** of an umbrella is that it is portable.
- The **benefit** is that you are free to go anywhere without the fear of getting wet.

If I were selling this book to you, I would have asked in the 'probe' part of the sales call what you looked for in a reference book. You may well have said:

"A reference book has to be durable so I can refer to it when I need to in the future."

I may have asked you also how important it is to be able to understand the technical points or jargon made in a reference book. You may have replied:

"I need to become familiar with the jargon and so it has to be explained clearly."

Then I may have asked you about how you use a reference book. You may have replied:

"I will pick it up and put it down depending on my needs. I will need to be able to quickly look something up without having to scour each and every page for the right information."

To summarise, the three main needs are as follows.

1. Durability.
2. Explanation of jargon.
3. Ease of reference.

I would then use a checking question. I would ask if there was anything else that we should consider before we move on – and if there wasn't anything, I would begin to talk about my product, carefully choosing the right features and benefits that will satisfy the above needs.

The first one is as follows:

- A **feature** about this book is that it has a cover and strong binding.
- The **benefit** is that the information inside will be protected and so the book can easily be used again and again.

The second:

- Another **feature** about this book is that is has a glossary of terms.
- The **benefit** is that the user can become familiar with sector jargon and terminology.

And the third:

- Another **feature** about this book is that it has chapters.
- The **benefit** is that you are able to access the right information at a glance, thus saving you time.

All sales training states that we have to explain the benefits to the customer and not the features. A customer probably doesn't care that a car has traction control but they do care that this means they are less likely to have an accident. A customer isn't bothered whether or not the chair is black but they become more interested if it is explained to them that this means dirt and stains are less likely to show up.

Highlighted in the boxes on the following pages are some typical features and benefits that could be used in a media advertisement sales role. I have provided a selection related to the various types of media being sold.

B2B Magazine – Features & Benefits

FEATURE	BENEFIT
The magazine is published weekly.	Advertising can begin working virtually straight away – saves time.
The magazine contains up to the minute news and features.	Attentive readership increases the opportunity to create an impact.
The magazine has a circulation of 10,000 key decision-making budget holders.	No wastage. Targeted advertising means optimum value for money.
We have a designated and easy to find 'jobs section'.	Readers know it's there so always check even if they're not actively looking – providing the best reach to potential candidates.
There are over 300 jobs featured every week, 20% are senior roles.	The highest number of professionals in the market use this product, ensuring vacancies are filled quickly.
The magazine employs 30% more writers and journalists than its nearest competitor.	Greater depth of coverage means readers place higher value on the product. Advertisers therefore reach a highly attentive audience which is likely to generate a higher quality response.

Consumer Magazine – Features & Benefits

FEATURE	BENEFIT
The magazine is monthly.	You will be spreading your advertising message for four weeks – optimum value for money / longer shelf life.
58% of copies are sold in London and the Home Counties.	Providing advertisers access to customers with a high disposable income brings the greatest sales potential.
The magazine has the highest volume of leading brands as advertisers than any other title in this market.	Those reading are receptive to lifestyle advertising leading to the strongest opportunity to influence your target group.
The audited circulation is 754,661, AB1 females aged between 25-34.	The highest concentration of this target group available means a huge reduction in wastage.
The circulation has grown 6.5% since last year.	This presents an opportunity for advertisers to reach new customers.
The average time taken by consumers to read this magazine is 120 minutes each month.	This presents an opportunity to really get in front of the right people and increase your market share.

Selling online – Features & Benefits

FEATURE	BENEFIT
Information & stories accessible 24/7.	Highest and unlimited exposure potential to target audience.
CTR (click-through rate) for advertisements is 3%.	Highest in market. Provides the best return on investment in this sector.
All display advertising is content matched.	Advertising impact amplified through reaching attentive and participative customers.
All advertisers provided with web support to change/adjust their campaigns.	Real-time response, fast and effective. Reacting to customer interest immediately.
Provides stand alone marketing or support to existing print campaigns.	Extending reach and market penetration – existing and new customers.
No print design and production costs, instantly adjustable creative, reactive to competition.	Cost-effective, agile advertising medium.

One interesting observation pertaining to all three example tables is that the benefits, although different in origination, allude to the same things. The benefits are almost interchangeable. Media salespeople should aim at proving, conclusively, that their product gives the client the best opportunity to achieve whatever it is they want to achieve, better than any other product around.

Broadly speaking, clients who are considering advertising in a b2b magazine, website or consumer publication need to generate a quick response as cost-effectively as possible, and perhaps ensure that the advertising makes a contribution towards the branding of the company. The effective use of features and benefits will help convince the client that they should proceed with placing some advertising. F&Bs have to be tailored to the needs of the customer, which are learned during the probe. The sales process is illustrated below:

Sales Process

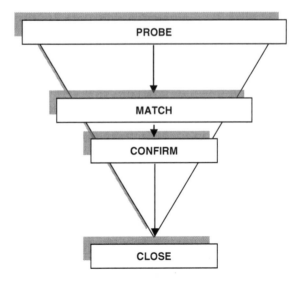

We begin by asking questions to find out what the client is looking to achieve. This is described as the **'probe'**. Probing is more than simply asking a few questions (which can sound interrogational). It involves having a two-way conversation and sharing 'airtime' aimed at achieving rapport as well as information that can lead to a sale. We listen and react to what is being said and try to interweave our questions into the conversation appropriately. When we feel we have gathered enough information, we can **summarise** the key points. Summaries can help in other ways too. For example you will be aware that conversations are prone to wandering off subject from time to time. To a degree we should allow this to happen in selling. If a client is reminded of an amusing anecdote concerning a farm animal and a fountain pen, then who are we to stop them from sharing that with us? It could help strengthen the relationship – something in common, perhaps. However, we need to be able to control the sometimes banal ramblings of bored clients, and a summary can help us do this. Having been entertained by an aside, we can regain conversational control by summarising the key points. This brings the call back to the main point. For example,

Salesperson: *"Really? I didn't think that would be possible with a fountain pen. Amazing. Now before I get confused, can I quickly summarise your needs so we're clear?"*

A polite confirmation of their ability to entertain followed by an appropriate statement to conclude that element of the conversation and then into the summary and back to making a sale.

Once we have understood the needs and summarised, we need to ask one more question before we can tailor our solution using the Features and Benefits. A **checking question,** as previously mentioned, is asked to capture any additional information that may be relevant that we haven't covered. For example,

Salesperson: *"Before I explain a bit more about our product, can I just check – is there anything else we should discuss or any other points to mention?"*

97

The reason this is a good idea is because we can't spend all day asking questions when we really only need the basics. However, if there is something important that the client feels might be relevant, then this is the opportunity for them to tell us. There might be some additional information they would like to share or not but the point is, if you don't ask it, you will never know.

Having probed, summarised and asked our checking question, we can then prove how our product can deliver the goals and close the deal. This stage is referred to as the **'match'** and uses the Features and Benefits. As we progress, we are asking for **'confirmation'** that the client understands or sees the value we can provide. We are increasing overall control of the call and we are moving progressively towards the **'close'**. The confirmation ensures that the two-way conversation continues throughout the sale, and reduces the likelihood of lecturing the client on endless features and benefits. Once we've matched the needs with our product benefits, we can comfortably and confidently ask for the order. Every move we make, every question we ask, should be aimed at moving further down the process towards our goal.

But how long does all this take? The answer is irritatingly predictable: it depends. It depends on how good the relationship is between the seller and the buyer, whether or not the buyer is able to proceed at that time and whether or not the buyer is convinced the product you are offering is the right one. So the process of closing a sale can take a single call, a few calls or months of hard work. As I said, it depends. The point is to keep on track and work your way through the process with each client. One thing is for sure – if you skip any part of the process, you won't get the sale.

Using F&Bs is a great way to explain how excellent our product is in the context of the client's needs. We do need to ensure, however, that the client is not excluded from the sales conversation during this part. Drowning clients in product talk is not ideal and should be avoided. We need to punctuate product description and continue to build commitment from the client. To achieve this we can use the third element to the sale which is **confirmation**, as referred to above.

Confirmation should occur when the salesperson feels it is appropriate to bring the client back in. It works as follows.

Salesperson: *"This magazine is published weekly."* *(Feature)*

"This means our clients find their advertisement begins working virtually straight away so the return on investment is faster." (Benefit)

"Does this sound as though it would be beneficial?" (Confirmation)

In any business, a quick return on investment would indeed be beneficial. His response therefore is likely to be positive. Confirmations help to maintain the conversational element to the sales process as well as ensuring the client understands and agrees to the benefits as we progress. If we collect 'yesses' following each F&B the client becomes used to agreeing, which may help us when we finally ask for the order.

A few more examples

Salesperson: *"As it is published weekly, the magazine contains up to the minute news." (Feature)*

"This means advertisers are appealing to a very attentive readership which increases the opportunity to create an impact." (Benefit)

"Do you see how that can work?"(Confirmation)

Salesperson: *"Our website has a CTR of 3."* **(Feature)**

"So this means advertisers receive the highest potential return on investment available in the market." **(Benefit)**

"Would that be useful in your situation?" **(Confirmation)**

Salesperson: *"The circulation has risen by 6.5% year on year."* **(Feature)**

"So this means advertisers are able to reach new customers, creating an opportunity to generate more sales." **(Benefit)**

"How would that support lead generation in other areas?" **(Confirmation)**

To put it simply, you ask the questions to find out what the prospect wants. You then **match** their needs to your product and when that is complete, you can see if they would like to proceed.

Following matching, you can strengthen the sale a bit further by **summarising** their needs and mentioning again how well your product can provide the most ideal solution. Whether you choose to do this depends on how the conversation has progressed. Sales conversations may go off in different directions, which is not a bad thing as most of the time 'chat' helps build relationships. A summary helps salespeople to bring the conversation back to the main purpose of the call.

14. Coping with objections

An objection can arise at any point during the sales process. For these purposes an 'objection' is anything the client believes prevents him or her from proceeding. Objections are frequent in selling but are not usually all that inspired so we can learn to deal with them effectively. There may be genuine and insurmountable reasons why a client is not going to buy advertising – and, short of blackmail and death threats, there is little we can do about these – but we can deal with many of the more standard objections, and this chapter discusses how.

It is perfectly usual for clients to proffer counter-arguments during the sale. For example, we may explain that the readership or user-base of our product exactly reflects the types of people they need to reach, which means if they were to advertise it would be very cost-effective. They may then point out that they could reach even more people by using a different medium and therefore improve cost-effectiveness further still.

This is less an objection and more of an opinion-based counter-argument that requires correction. We can explain that it is possible to reach many more people using all sorts of methods but the objective is to reach the right people and not just a lot of people. If they were to choose the higher-volume route, they would probably find it to be significantly less cost-effective.

The strategy here is not to disagree with clients but to remind them of the key objectives that we have established earlier in the call. In actual fact, we can agree with a client that what they say makes sense but, looked at from a different perspective, could lead to a different conclusion. A scooter is indeed cheaper than an estate car but if you want to transport an entire family, which is the better option?

When faced with a counter-argument, we should aim to do the following:

- Fully understand the point they are making.
- Deal with it non-defensively.
- Offer a logically sound and reasonable alternative view.

101

These moves are the underlying principles to dealing with objections.

If a client sees the cost as a barrier, we need to put the price in perspective, which helps convince clients as to the value they will get. Here are a few typical objections and ideas about how to cope.

"It's too expensive"

Generally, it is wise to remember that most buyers will claim the first price to be too high in the hope that we will lower it. If we expect buyers to complain about the price initially, we should always go in higher in anticipation. Simple, really.

If a client claims our price is too high we need to find out if this is in comparison to their budget or to another offer they've had elsewhere. Ideas as to how to deal with the question of budget are outlined below.

"Budget too low"

If their objection is related to budget, we have two options. The first is to recap the main objectives to the advertising and persuade them to reconsider. The fact is that if a business stands still, others will overtake it. Advertising in whatever form is the best way to sustain credibility with existing customers as well as create new ones and open up new markets.

Our second option is to lower the price. The golden rule on this is if the price goes down, so does the proposal. The price and the package are adjusted together or not at all. By this I mean if they are offered a half page for £700 but only have £350 to spend, we do not negotiate down on the price without reducing the size of the advertisement. So for £350 they can buy a quarter page. If we can't persuade them to spend the larger amount, we need to fit the package to the available funds. If they want the larger advertisement for a price that is unacceptable to us, then we simply decline the offer. A bad deal is worse than no deal, in that lowering prices sets precedents for future deals. I maintain that if a customer has a need to buy but thinks the product is too expensive, then they have not been made aware of the true value of the product. In media sales it is very common to speak regularly to the same advertiser, therefore it is crucial to ensure we set the rules of engagement at the outset.

"Competitor is cheaper"

If the price objection is related to a competitor offering a lower rate, my response would be that very few things in life can be fairly compared on price alone. To use a previous analogy, is a scooter better than an estate car simply because it is cheaper? Should we buy a house in Bratislava because it is cheaper than Birmingham? Analogies to clarify the point you want to make are a useful and illustrative method of persuasion.

In the majority of cases, if you pay less you get less. When this objection has been raised on training courses, I have suggested that we can challenge clients on the basis that if they are sure the competition has exactly the same editorial quality, the same relationship with their readers and can offer access to precisely the same potential customers *for less money*, then they should use the competition.

One of the most useful and illustrative questions we can ask a client when faced with a price objection is whether they are after the *best price* or the *lowest price*. This question raises the issue of value. It is a bit like asking whether they want a discount or to solve their marketing problem.

Take a moment here and try to name any product in life which you buy purely by how much it costs...Any luck?

You may have thought of basic products like ballpoint pens, string or light bulbs, which to some degree are bought on price but even with these purchases very often other factors are considered.

If we are taking the pet cat to the vet, for example, we may well need some string to ensure it doesn't fall off the roof of the car. As a result, we may consider which colour would suit both the cat and the car, how much string we are going to need as well as the strength of the twine. If we consider so many factors for such a minor purchase why would we determine where to advertise our company purely based on how much it costs?

If the client is adamant they are only interested in the cheapest option we could suggest they consider advertising in The Beano. While this magazine is predominantly (although not exclusively) read by children, it is likely to be cheaper than a leading consumer magazine. Although this is a relatively high-risk strategy, it makes the point that accuracy of readership is another, perhaps more important consideration than how much it costs. One can always get something cheaper, but will it do the job?

As salespeople, it is vital that we know the differences between our own product and any competitive products. If we are unable to explain conclusively why we are charging more, then we may as well give up. The American author, Mark Twain said: *"Few things in life are harder to put up with than the annoyance of a good example."*

Meaning if someone is conclusively right about something during a debate, it can certainly be annoying but also that the debate is over.

So "the competition is cheaper" can be dealt with by explaining that no two media products are the same and so can never truly be compared. They will represent a market in different ways and can achieve different results. The skill is in knowing what the differences are and being able to explain them to justify the price differential.

There's a golden rule emerging here, which is to know more about the competition than your clients – then the odds will be very much more in your favour.

"It doesn't work"

Another classic objection in media sales is when the client believes the advertisement, or advertising in general, doesn't actually make a difference. Clients often gauge success or failure by the amount of response they receive as a result of advertising in a magazine or website. By 'response', we mean how many customers make an enquiry to the advertiser following placement of an advertisement on a website or in a magazine. While some clients do not manage to generate much response with their advertisements for reasons discussed later on, it is equally true that many do and are very happy with the result.

This is moderately reasonable for anyone placing an advertisement for recruitment purposes. If a client places an advertisement for a marketing manager in a marketing magazine or recruitment website, they will judge the success of failure of their investment by how many applications they receive. They often restrict their advertising frequency to one or two weeks due to the negative signal being sent if a job is advertised for longer.

For 'services' classified sections of magazines or websites, this is perhaps less realistic. An advertiser looking to generate new interest in his service or product may place an advertisement in good faith. He patiently waits by the phone in anticipation of a deluge of new business enquiries and, after a few days, the telephone has begun to gather dust. He occasionally checks the ringer still works but slowly becomes disillusioned. In time, we call to see how things are going and whether or not he would like to book another advertisement. The following tirade of abuse can make even students blush or maybe their response is that we hear nothing but sad resignation to the fact that this has been as predicted, another huge waste of company resource.

Our reaction is first to empathise with the client's view. We can genuinely appreciate that to have spent an amount of money on advertising and yet received little or no outcome would indeed be disappointing. The problem is that clients immediately blame the medium for their advertisement's apparent failure.

This means our next job is to try to reassure them that they made the right decision to buy an advertisement in our product and that the problem must lie elsewhere.

We can recap on the reasons why they chose this particular magazine, which may have been:

- It is read by the right type of individuals.
- It is representative of the size of the market.
- The editorial content has an excellent reputation.

The fact is that at the time they bought the advertisement, our product ticked all the above boxes and still does, so the problem is unlikely to be related to where they placed the advertisement.

We are trying to suggest that if something doesn't work, don't throw it away but try to fix it instead. If their car breaks down they wouldn't just chuck the key in a ditch and buy another one, they would find out what went wrong and get it repaired.

We need to help the advertiser understand what could have gone wrong. Here are a number of factors to consider:

105

- The advertisement may have been too small.
- The design may not have been attractive enough.
- They may have advertised at a difficult time of year.
- There may be considerable competition in this area.
- They may have only placed one or two advertisements which were not enough to generate and sustain interest.
- They may not have had very many ways for prospective customers to contact the advertising company.
- Maybe the product or vacancy only appealed to a small number of people and therefore a limited or negligible response was inevitable.

Discussion of these often helps to placate a frustrated advertiser and may even convince them to place another, perhaps larger advertisement.

Then of course there's the real reason why it didn't generate any response. Trying to measure advertising effectiveness purely by response is oversimplifying the process. Even the magic measuring of web traffic can lead us to oversell the capability of advertising. As an example, let's look at two similar sized companies with different marketing strategies.

Company A
Marketing strategy – Place a single ½ page colour ad in 25 issues of a magazine and on an associated website.

Cost: £35,000
Outcome: No direct response.

Company B
Marketing strategy – Never advertise.

Cost: nil
Outcome: No direct response.

Which is the better plan? Here, the answer is Company B as they got the same result but spent nothing. Then look at it using other points of comparison:

Company A
New customers up by 6%
Existing customers business up by 8.4%
Operating profit up by 1.6%
Overall cost of advertising: £35,000

Company B
New customers nil
Existing customer business down by 6%
Operating profit down by 1.3%
Overall cost of advertising: Nil

The point is that advertising cannot simply be measured by how many people actually respond to the advertisement. Advertising has to be seen as an investment with every type of advertising contributing to overall organisational growth. The only reason we turn up at an exhibition for example, is because we read about it in a magazine or saw it on the net – or we may have been told about it by a friend, suggesting that word of mouth is stronger than advertising. However, if you want people to pass on the word, then you have to give it to them in the first place and advertising is the only way to do that.

It may be true that the advertising company's results show that a large proportion of new business originates from their presence at an exhibition, which if compared makes the other forms of advertising seem to contribute very little. This outcome may suggest the company should discontinue with 'unsuccessful' forms of advertising and instead concentrate on the exhibitions. This means when the media salesperson calls to sell press advertising space, the client may claim that 'it doesn't work'.

They may explain that their strategy has meant a decision to cancel any plans to use press and any further development of their website because they have found exhibitions work far better for them. If only life was this simple! On my sales courses, I explain that there are basically two types of purchase: impulse and protracted.

Impulse purchases are things like chocolate bars, newspapers, drinks, etc. They are those products we need very little consideration before deciding to purchase.

Protracted purchases are those that take far more consideration. Things like cars, houses, insurance policies, clothes, which sports club to join, which companies to contract, etc.

A potential customer looking to secure the services of an accountancy or law firm, or a consumer looking to buy some garden furniture or a new car will inevitably need more time to decide. This suggests that most products and services advertised in b2b and consumer media are in the 'protracted' category. Typical customers of any 'protracted' product purchase will go through five primary decision-making stages which are:

1. Identification of the problem faced.
2. Analysis of solution options available in the market.
3. Shortlist of potential suppliers.
4. Purchase of service or product that will hopefully resolve the problem.
5. Post-mortem – is life better now?

Buying a new car, for example...

1. The problem is I can't get to the train station.
2. My options are: bike, scooter, car, camel, tele-transportation device.
3. Appropriate options or shortlist: scooter/car.
4. Bought car.
5. Life improved.

The period of time this takes varies. Deciding which sports club to join will obviously take less time than deciding which airline to buy but both decisions will have these stages in evidence.

As advertisers are selling their 'solution' to the customer, they have to ensure their product or service is in front of potential customers as much as possible. It may well be that the channel through which most contracts are secured happens to be an exhibition, but this simply means that the combination of all types of media being used has been successful, and not simply that exhibitions work and the rest is a waste of money. When a client places an advertisement in any form of advertising vehicle they are not actually buying customers or even potential response. They are buying the opportunity to INFLUENCE their target market. In the illustration below the chap is a reader of a magazine or viewer of a website and therefore a potential customer to our advertisers. When an advertisement is placed in a magazine or on a website the advertisement appears in front of that potential customer and begins to influence them.

If he doesn't respond to the advertising message, however, the advertiser can become frustrated and often blames the advertising vehicle – hence *'it doesn't work'*. The point is that advertising cannot be fairly measured by the amount of direct response and that the reality is that magazines, websites, supplements, exhibitions, conferences, trade shows, inserts and consumer direct mail all offer the opportunity to *influence* customers and do not give advertisers the right to expect a deluge of new business.

As I mentioned, this is a fair and accurate assessment of the actual function of the media from a product or service advertising perspective, though for reasons already explained it is less appropriate for recruitment advertisers. It is a fact that magazines and websites are an excellent access point for available vacancies in various sectors. A good b2b magazine for example will have about 80% of all available jobs in that sector advertised at the back. This means that if someone is looking for a design-related job they will look in *Design Week*, if they are looking for a marketing position they will look in *Marketing Week,* and so on. If an advertiser complains about the lack of response to their recruitment advertisements we can look to use similar arguments such as:

- *Maybe there were lots of similar jobs advertised at the same time (possibly at higher salaries).*
- *Maybe the advertisement failed to mention the salary details to entice applicants.*
- *Maybe it was a slow time of year (December is slow for recruitment as people generally prefer to wait until after Christmas to look for a new job).*
- *Maybe the advertisement was too small/lacked detail/ unattractive etc*

Of course, it also depends on the type of vacancy being advertised. If the role is very senior, there are obviously fewer potential applicants who can apply, or if it is a junior position maybe there is too much choice. Whatever the reason, it is unlikely to be the magazine or website that is at fault if it has been proven that the readership corresponds to those appropriate for the advertised role.

There is also the point about whether the vacancy appeals to 'browsers' or 'seekers'. These are reader types of b2b magazines or websites. A **browser** is an employed individual not actively looking for a new position. They may, however, be influenced if something good comes up. A **seeker**, on the other hand, is someone who is actively looking for a job.

To convince a 'browser' to apply, the advertisement must be strong enough to persuade them to take action. Again, if the response is limited – is it the magazine's or website's fault, or is it that the advertisement itself has failed in some way? A media sales executive would do well to remember that the contract they have agreed with an advertiser is to provide access to their target group and not to generate response. We fulfil our end of the bargain and nothing in life can give companies a fast track to new business.

In conclusion, I might add that advertising *does* work. It is, however, a complicated process and one that can rarely be quantified – except perhaps in the case of online advertisements. Nowadays website operators are able to find out what the viewing figures are on advertisements placed through accessing data available on the server. They are also able to provide information to advertisers and media owners on 'dwell-time' which describes the quantity of time users spend on a website. So more precise methods of measurement on the effectiveness of online advertising are already there and have become a huge selling point for media owners and an identified benefit which advertisers will come to expect. Nevertheless, measuring web activity is still relatively basic and continues to be the subject of much debate. So for now, advertising success can only really be measured by overall growth.

"We don't need to advertise"

If you are responsible for selling recruitment advertising space, you will not be able to sell anything if the company to whom you are talking is not currently recruiting. Hence this objection relates to those advertisers that provide a product or service and are not looking to advertise a vacancy.

'Today's advertising is tomorrow's business' is relevant here. Here's another useful adage: *'The man who stops advertising to save money, is the same man that stops a clock to save time.'*

The first saying warns us against complacency. Resting on one's laurels, as it were, risks future success – and, as we have said, advertising creates awareness which influences buying decisions. Deciding not to advertise will guarantee customer activity reduces to nil.

The second saying similarly underscores the need to take a long-term view before dismissing the value of advertising.

Consider the following customer attributes:

- Customers tell us what products they need.
- Customers tell us how and when they want to buy.
- Customers tell us how much they can afford.
- Customers tell us how we compare with our competitors.
- Customers tell us how we can improve and evolve our product.
- Customers introduce and advertise our products to other customers.

So it appears that limiting contact with customers is not a particularly good plan – and *not* advertising is doing just that. Sure as ice is cold, if you stop telling people how brilliant something is, it won't be long before they begin to think something else is brilliant instead. From a profit perspective, it is reckoned that it costs something like five times as much to regain lost market share as it does to get it in the first place. As you have probably gathered, my view is that in order to prosper, any company has to continue advertising, and should always devote a proportion of profit or turnover to just that, however small.

"We only buy pay-per-click campaigns"

Having bought space on a commercial website promising to reach his customers, the advertiser will pay an amount of money each time someone clicks on his advertisement. This is instead of paying a one-off rate upfront. This appears an attractive alternative to a fixed fee because the advertiser is apparently only paying for the response they actually receive. If you are selling against this, the way to approach it is by explaining to the advertiser that actually, this is far from an ideal arrangement. The problem is the imbalance of interest. The publishing company (and sales executive) are paid according to the level of click-through and the publishing company has influence over this level. I am not suggesting that any media owner will deliberately falsify click-though rates but quite plainly it is possible, and so risk is undeniably evident. No, it is far more sensible to pay an agreed price for something that is proven and reliable, without any risk. Pay-per-click is similar to sponsoring a charity walk on a per mile rate but without knowing the distance. It's all a bit risky and what seemed a good idea at the time could cost a fortune and yet still not yield the anticipated level of business. My advice to advertisers is to buy from the most reputable source, check and double-check the statistics being quoted and pay the price.

"We're maintaining existing business, not looking for new customers"

It is hard to believe, I know, but this objection does crop up, and is particularly evident in the current economic climate. The theory is that due to the recession there are fewer active customers out there, so it appears that advertising to try and secure their business is pointless. It is true that there are fewer new customers out there, but it is also true that everyone is open to a better deal, if one were to be offered. Supplier loyalty has gone out of the window at the moment, which means that any company still advertising has the metaphorical ear of its competitor's customers for the first time in years. What a fantastic opportunity! Relying on existing business and ceasing to advertise at the moment is certainly not the answer. This issue covered in more detail later on in Chapter 16.

There are many other objections that can arise – perhaps the advertiser doesn't like the layout of the magazine, or perhaps the editorial office have written a negative piece about the advertiser – but the general rule continues to apply: agree with their logic; try to see it from their perspective; then offer a compensating alternative view.

As long as the magazine reaches the right people and represents the size of the market, very little else matters.

15. Closing the sale

Some folk would have it that this is the hardest part of the sales process. My view is that it's like a bicycle – as I have found so many things are in life – in that if you've got the right parts and put them all together in the right order and in the right way, then there is a pretty good chance it will work. So closing is less 'the final step' and more the culmination of a number of steps successfully undertaken. The right to ask for the order only emerges if you have understood the needs and matched them and attained client agreement along the way. Having reached the point of asking for the order means you have successfully probed, matched and gained the client's understanding and agreement.

In a previous chapter I mentioned that sales managers have asked me to help salespeople with their closing skills and after a little investigation it emerges that while they may be able to *ask* for the order, they are failing to understand the needs and match with benefits before doing so. Anyone can physically ask for an order but only the brave and true can do it at the right time. This is less of a textbook solution than some might think as it all depends on your own judgement. Unlike those scripted sales operations, in this business the sales managers hand over the responsibility and authority to you as a salesperson to handle the deal from start to finish. You will, of course, have access to on-the-job advice, sales training and books to help hone your techniques, but unless you can feel when it is right to close you may have a little trouble doing it. It's a bit like knowing where the fish are before you put in the line, in that a bit of experience will tell us the right time and the right place to catch the most fish.

To help get the feel, it is useful to be able to spot the psychological turning point of the customer. The things we should look out for are often reflected in our own behaviour. How do you usually feel when you have decided to go ahead and buy something? You may feel differently towards buying a new set of pencils than, say, confirming a six-month holiday in the Bahamas with a celebrity partner of your choice but, however you feel, it is likely to create a change in behaviour. Although body language tends to be the dominant factor in communication, this is hardly reliable when talking to someone over the phone. Instead, we can rely on *tonal delivery*, which reflects the emotional status of an individual. The voice is a good determinant of how we feel about something in that tone, pitch, rhythm, volume and inflection all contribute to communicating feelings.

Even buying advertising space can invoke an emotional response of some kind. Buying from someone might create a sense of power, which generates a good feeling. While buying advertising space may not necessarily create happiness, it may mean the buyer is able to tick off another job, which will probably make them feel pleasure. Alternatively, agreeing to buy advertising space may mean the client has completed this part of a marketing plan, which again will make them feel good. They may even feel pleased they have finally come to a decision.

Signs you may notice might be when the conversation begins to include indications of the customer's agreement (and even examples *from them*) as to where buying may help in other ways. Customers who have subconsciously decided to buy begin to think and talk 'post-purchase'. They may ask about invoicing deadlines, or who else is advertising in that section, the date of publication and so on. Another obvious sign is a gradual reduction in resistance. Customers who begin to say less as the benefits are explained are not so much being bored by the experience as growing perhaps more convinced they should proceed. These are all indicators that clients are willing to say yes, and occur due to an emotional change. As a result, it is time to ask for the business. This is one of the reasons why listening is so important in selling. We listen for an explanation of needs but also to hear their emotional gear changes.

When you feel it is right to ask for the business you should go ahead and do it. Avoid procrastination and deferment and get on with it. The worst that can happen is they say 'no'. This is never a bad thing as at least they have considered buying, which is more than they were doing before you came along.

You can use the '**optional**' close:
Would you prefer a quarter or half of a page?
Would you prefer a series of three advertisements or six?

Would you prefer to go online and print or begin with online alone?

This ensures the client is thinking of *what* he should buy as opposed to whether or not he should buy. It strengthens the sale by demonstrating how much you believe this is the perfect solution.

You could make a deliberate error to line up an 'Optional' close:

Salesperson:	*"You mentioned the product is being launched in July." (Deliberate error)*
Client:	*"No, it's in May!"*
Salesperson:	*"Oh right, so the best time to start advertising would be April then?"*
Client:	*"Yes."*
Salesperson:	*"Half or full page d'you think?" (Optional close)*

Another is the **'assumptive'**:

If the sale has gone well and the client has indicated interest, we can assume they want to proceed:

Client:	*"Yes, it sounds good."*
Salesperson:	*"In that case, let's go with the quarter page at £400 starting in the next issue. Would you like me to include the right-hand-side position as well?"*

This has assumed the client wants to go ahead and that it is merely the details that have to be discussed.

The **'illustrative'** close helps clients visualise what they will get as a result of buying an advertisement. I think most of us like to see what we get before we buy but, in the case of advertising space, apart from sending them a copy of the magazine or giving them a website address to review, this is not possible. We cannot physically introduce clients to the readers and so must rely instead on our clients trusting the statistics and what we tell them. For some this might appear a bit too difficult. So the illustrative close works as follows:

Salesperson:	*"Would you like to confirm the booking?"*
Client:	*"I'm not sure... maybe I should think about it."*
Salesperson:	*"If you decided to go ahead, what size advertisement would you go for?"*
Client:	*"Well if I do, I'd probably have a small one."*
Salesperson:	*"A ¼ page perhaps, using your company's Royal Blue corporate colour round the edge?"*
Client:	*"Um...could do."*
Salesperson:	*"That would look great. Where would you put the logo? At the top right corner? Or bottom left?"*
Client:	*"Top middle to make it stand out I think."*

Discuss a few more features of the advertisement to clearly get the image in the client's mind and then go for another close. The idea is to get the client to see what he is buying to make it more tangible. He may say 'yes', or he may still want to delay but at least you have pushed as hard as possible to get the deal.

Using the **'rebound'** technique protects the sale from being soured by talk of prices too early in the call. A client asking the price of advertising towards the end of the discussion is fine as it signals readiness to discuss a deal. Giving prices too early will cloud the client's decision to proceed. In this case, clients may well subconsciously compare one advertising option with another and choose the cheapest. It is our job to ensure they know the value of our offer before we discuss prices so the price seems fair compared to what is on offer elsewhere. A rebound close works as follows:

Client:	*"So, how much does it cost to advertise?"*
Salesperson:	*"That depends. What size advertisement are you interested in booking?"*

Answering a question with a question protects us from having to divulge too much of the wrong information too early. If the client persists, however, it is better to provide a selection of prices than continue to baulk. However, bear in mind that if someone were to ask how much a house was in the North East of England, it would be difficult to answer without knowing more about their precise needs. The same is true with advertising space. The costs do vary enormously and so if we can get a few more needs before we quote prices, so much the better.

The **'profit v loss'** close should be used with care and applied if the relationship and sale thus far is strong enough. It works like this:

Salesperson:	*"Would you like to go ahead with the three quarter-pages as we discussed?"*
Client:	*"I'm not sure I can afford to at the moment. Maybe later in the year."*
Salesperson:	*"I understand. But the longer it's left, the more opportunity there is for others to take market share. It takes time to build business and the earlier the start the quicker the return."*

Nothing can guarantee to turn a client around but our job is to persuade by pointing out the benefits of buying today. We have to try everything within reason to push through to close and, in the example, there is a real risk of clients losing out on market share if advertising is delayed. This argument presents a logical and perhaps thought-provoking viewpoint.

The **'puppy dog'** close is another option. This is begging pure and simple and, in some cases, dependent on the customer relationship can work very well. It works like this:

119

Salesperson:	*"I've got one quarter page left before I can go home and if I don't sell it, I won't get my monthly commission! Will you take it off my hands?"*
Client:	*"Well, um. I'm not sure we have the budget at the moment."*
Salesperson:	*"Oh go on, please. You know it's worth it and it would make my day if you did."*

Notice the complete lack of benefits or any type of structure! A puppy dog close relies on the goodwill of known clients and should only be used on occasion and only with clients where there is a good relationship.

At the point of closing deals one extra element will yet again strengthen the prospect of securing a deal. The **'pause'** is a classic technique used by experienced sellers. Once the sale process has been applied, the crunch time arrives and we ask for the order. Following a proposal, the salesperson should shut up and wait. It works like this:

Salesperson:	*"So I suggest a series of six quarter-page advertisements starting from the next issue. Shall we go ahead?"*

The pause begins.

At this stage, the client *has* to be the next person to speak. If the salesperson continues talking, fearing a continued silence, they will dilute the power of the question. This will inevitably be felt by the client and risks a negative response. Our delivery has to convey complete belief in the idea and total confidence this is precisely the right solution.

I have been in sales situations where, having asked for the business, the silence appears to last for hours! Of course it is only ever a few seconds but at this stage of the sale, it can seem like a lifetime.

During the pause stage, the client is weighing up the pros and cons of the opportunity and feels under pressure to make a decision. They may be feeling a number of mixed emotions at this point, which may include worrying about having to come up with a totally convincing argument *not* to buy, or the risk of showing cowardice if they say no or even concern about facing any disappointment from the seller. This is all good! After all – we are convinced they should buy and so should they be!

The choice of how we close cannot realistically be predetermined. It has to fit the nature of the call and this is down to personal judgement. In many role-plays I have conducted with salespeople it has been the interaction that has determined the close. A salesperson may not be aware that they applied an optional close until I mention it afterwards, which suggests they are being intuitive, listening, gauging the relationship and making choices as to how best to proceed. As I mentioned, there is one guarantee in selling: if you fail to close, you will not get any business.

One last consideration to bear in mind with regard to closing a media deal, is that there are six primary reasons why people buy and these are captured, unsurprisingly, in an acronym:

S.P.A.C.E.R.

S – Security
Is the product well known? Is it a recognised brand? Who else has bought it?

P – Performance
Does it actually work? How do I know? Where's the evidence? Have I been convinced?

A – Appearance
If I buy this, what is the risk of looking a fool? Will it increase my standing in the company?

C – Convenience

How much work do I have to do to get this? Does it fit with other areas of activity? Is it compatible or am I going to have to change everything else to accommodate it?

E – Economic

Does it provide good value? Can I afford it?

R – Relationship

Do I like the company selling it? Do I respect the seller? Do I trust them?

If all these aspects have been addressed during the sale, the likelihood of getting a deal is vastly increased. Interestingly, if you take another look at these, you may notice that with the possible exception of 'Economic' all the other reasons for purchase are based on an emotion – how someone feels – which provides an important insight into how to successfully close a deal. Appeal to the feelings as well as to the reason – and judge the time to close based on how the customer seems to be feeling, as well as what they are saying.

16. Selling in a downturn

In the UK the retail price index which includes mortgage payments has fallen beyond all expectation and is at the lowest rate since the early 1960s. Food prices are up 11% from last year and gas and electricity bills have increased by about 35%. The slump and continued decline in house valuations is estimated to wipe out any equity growth since 2003. (I worked out my estimated retirement age based against the current financial situation and it was 96 ¾.)

However, by comparison to the Great Depression in the 1930s, which witnessed over 10,000 banks fail, saw unemployment reach 25% and the GNP fall by 45%, things are looking pretty good.

Life is fairly interesting everywhere at the moment and not least for the media industry. Advertising revenues are always hit early on in a downturn (and I might add, always amongst the earliest to recover); they have reduced significantly across all media. In some areas of print publishing, revenues have dropped by over 50% leaving organisations reeling from the shock, concerned that it could worsen in the months ahead. Media owners across the industry are re-evaluating their portfolio and looking to make savings wherever possible and frantically trying to think of ways through the quagmire. With revenues so low, companies are finding themselves suddenly exposed and without much control over matters. Publishing houses that have invested in new or varied revenue streams and tried to limit their risk in other ways, will inevitably fair better. All media organisations are being hit at the moment and, inevitably, we will witness some fairly major industry adjustments as we move ahead.

As we discover later in this chapter, history tells us that during a downturn consumer behaviour changes. Customers who were formerly loyal to a specific brand are now open to the idea of switching providers to save a bit of money or get a bit more value. I was called by my broadband supplier last week and offered a reasonable discount if I was prepared to continue my contract for another year. Their strategy was to get in touch with their contracted customers a few months away from renewal and offer them a good enough deal to preserve the business. This had to happen before I started looking for a better offer, or one of their competitors got in touch. Some car manufacturers are offering an unbelievable two-for-one deal whereby if someone buys an SUV they get a city car free. I'm not suggesting that desperate discounting is a good strategy but it does demonstrate people and companies are being forced to think differently.

Media organisations need to adjust their strategy too. They need to look at ways to ring-fence existing customers wherever possible. This can include subscription offers, loyalty discounts, longer contract terms or crescendo contracts whereby the value increases the longer the contract has been running, to reduce the likelihood of cancellation – these also help to remind customers of the value they are receiving closer to renewal time. One very successful b2b publication decided to renew advertising contracts three months before they were due. This tactic pre-empted any counter-attack from the competitor and contractually locked in existing customers. Thinking ahead and thinking differently are absolutely central to success.

Another example is the fast food industry. According to their results, they are doing well at the moment, which is a direct reflection of changing behaviour. People still need to eat and enjoy life but are now cutting their cloth accordingly. Consumers have moved down a peg from more upmarket restaurant chains and family owned bistros to fulfil their lifestyle need but at reduced cost. During the depression of the 1930s, sales of cinema tickets soared, partly because movies cheered everyone up and had a pleasant social atmosphere but also because cinemas provided free heating.

Effectively we are all in the middle of an economic forest fire. Even ancient oaks can fall and some already have. Everyone will get singed to a greater or lesser extent, and, sadly, some won't make it out the other side. It's destructive and depressing. On the good side, all fires burn out eventually, and although it may appear a long way off, we're a lot closer to the end than we were last month. No grass roots but at least we can say the seeds are in the ground.

People under the age of thirty won't have experienced a recession before, so this is all very new to them. They will have been enjoying the good times of the last few years, and those who work in media sales will probably be quite shocked by the difficulty they are having selling advertising space.

Interestingly, a report compiled by WARC for the Advertising Association estimates that advertising expenditure will increase significantly over the next ten years with the internet being the primary driver. Print, too, is still very strong and has a rosy future. The PPA state that in 2008, around 230 new consumer magazines were launched with this market being worth around £3bn. The consumer magazine market is set to increase by just below 6% by 2012 despite the economic gloom. We are a nation that enjoys its magazines and if previous recessions are anything to go by, publications on hobbies actually manage to increase their circulations as more people seek refuge in the things they love most (and more people unexpectedly have the time to do so!). Not all is lost and there is no doubt the media industry will ultimately prosper as it always has.

But until we can comfortably get back to buying things we don't need, how do we sell advertising space in a downturn? There are some facts we should go through before I tell you the plan.

In a recession, the number of companies actively advertising reduces. In a large number of cases, those that do continue to advertise, reduce spend dramatically. Their customers are also reducing expenditure, which means any advertising that is placed is probably going to yield lower returns. Therefore it appears to make sense not to bother advertising.

Stay with this...

It is also true that people like you and I are open to changing their supplier or brand in order to make a saving, or increase the value. Our loyalty to our chosen brand or supplier reduces because we are feeling the pinch. House insurance is one example where customers simply choose the cheapest option and are more proactively doing so due to their situation. When cash is less of a problem, we are quite happy to sign the form on renewal day, with the current supplier. Not so in these darker days. This suggests that customers can be persuaded to leave their existing supplier in favour of another. At this point an opportunity presents itself for organisations small or large, to chip away at their competitors customer base. At what other time could a fast food outlet come close to persuading a Chelsea resident to buy a burger with or without cheese, or a BMW owner to consider a small economical Mazda? I am not saying there's anything wrong with either a burger or a Mazda – in fact, I've owned both in my time – but the reality is that companies are now able to target different customers. You may point out that if they were to target these new customers and successfully secure their business, it would merely replace the ones already lost, which is true. The benefits, however, are in the medium to long term. When the good times return, so does brand loyalty, and there's a good chance the former BMW owner who swapped to a smaller Mazda will want a larger car, and there's an excellent chance they will stay with the current brand.

This has positive implications for the media salesperson because it provides a way to get around the new objection of "it's the recession, we've stopped advertising."

If you think about it, this objection tends to put a full stop to even the most proficient pitch. When faced with this problem, we have two options. The first is to argue our case and metaphorically thump the client over the head with a few product benefits and hope they forget everything that's happened over the last few months. Or we can simply agree. In this situation, I'd go with the latter.

We cannot deny the recession exists and we are not able to bring it to a halt. Therefore it seems we have to go with it. Agreement with the client flatters them and supports their theory. They are pleased and relieved they don't have to defend their position. It also reduces the level of desperation the client feels to get us off the phone.

If we agree, then the problem of 'the recession' has been successfully removed as a direct point of difference. The next step is to replace it with a different problem. We do this by recounting something we have heard or read recently that the client may find interesting. The problem we need to talk about is the difficulty of customer retention during a downturn.

The following is an example of a 'bounce' conversation which I have broken down into seven stages, to correspond with the diagram on page 128:

1. Client:	*"It's the recession. We've stopped advertising."*
2. Salesperson:	*"Quite right. A lot of companies are doing this, actually. They need to control expenditure. I think you're doing the right thing."*
3. Client:	*"Oh good, right then. Well, sorry about that."*

(At this point the client is ending the sales call. The salesperson recognises this critical point and tries to move it back up the scale)

4. Salesperson:	*"Oh! I've just remembered an article I read the other day. You'd be interested in this... It was talking about how some organisations are losing their customers to smaller suppliers."*

(Point 4 – The salesperson has bounced the conversation away from an immovable problem and asks the client to consider an alternative view.)

5. Client:	*"I can imagine. It's awful."*

6. Salesperson: *"They reckoned it is due to these other companies using specific marketing methods to chip away at their bigger rivals. Do you know it costs five times as much to regain lost market share as it does to get it in the first place?"*

7. Client: *"No, I didn't know that. So what are these magical marketing methods?"*

Salesperson: *"Apparently, it's high-visibility, response-driven and low-cost targeting of the key decision buyers."*

Client: *"Really? What else did it say?"*

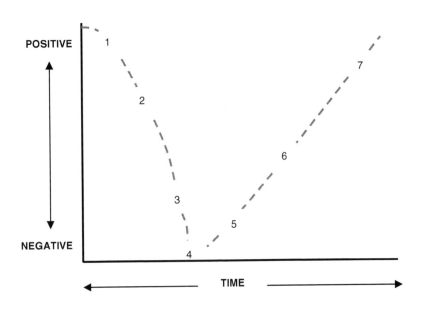

The conversation could have nose-dived and ended abruptly. However, with this method, the salesperson picks up the pace and injects a new perspective.

The conversation continues which is a success in itself. While it may not end in an order, the seed has been sown for future and more positive conversations.

In fact, the client's response in this conversational thread doesn't matter much at all. You have control of the conversation, topic, direction and pace, so it's less important how they respond. Your focus is on suggesting that they are practically instructing their customers to use another supplier, simply by not advertising. You have effectively bounced the conversation off the bottom by agreeing, and then gone into another problem that does have a solution.

The alternative is to make product benefits sound so fantastically attractive that they immediately overshadow economic meltdown. But this is a long shot if you haven't addressed the objection first. Better to deal with the objection logically and head-on before we get to the benefits, and the first thing to do is to admit it's there.

Another example using a different response from the client is as follows:

Client:	*"We've kept the website but due to the economy, we've had to stop advertising".*
Salesperson:	*"Oh, that's a shame. A lot of companies are taking this approach, though. They need to control expenditure. I think you're doing the right thing"*
Client:	*"Thanks for calling, though, and we'll look at it again in a few months."*
Salesperson:	*"Ok, no problem. I'll call again when things are improved. Actually, while you're on, I recently read an article on advertising during a recession. You'd be interested in this...It was talking about how some organisations are losing their customers to smaller suppliers."*

No reaction from the client...

(This lack of response suggests that although the client is not fully on board, they are prepared to listen)

Salesperson continues...:

	"They reckoned it is due to these other companies using specific marketing methods to chip away at their competitors. Do you know it costs five times as much to regain lost market share as it does to get it in the first place?"
Client:	*"I didn't. Spending anything on advertising at the moment is for the big boys only I'm afraid. The ones with all the spare cash."*
Salesperson:	*"I agree but they're not spending much either! But what they are doing is buying advertising that creates high visibility and high response at the lowest cost possible. They're actually taking customers away from anyone and everyone. Presumably you'd look at something like this. Would you like an example of how they're doing it?"*
Client:	*"Well, I'll look at it...."*

I was selling advertising during the 1990 downturn and clearly remember using this technique. I changed because I was getting nowhere and needed an alternative approach and this is just that, an *approach* and not an instant solution. We need a method to get clients to see things differently and this is the opening that has the highest success rate.

I'm not offering a guarantee but I am offering a suggestion as to how to fight back and fight harder. Hiding isn't the answer for business. In fact, communication with customers should be increased during a recession. Revenues will still be lower than this time last year, and there's not a lot we can do about that for now, but we can get a larger share of whatever is out there, by operating smarter. Those who are good at sales have more than one method of operation. They adjust their voice pitch, pace and approach to give them the best opportunity to secure business. The best of the best have numerous approaches according to the situation they face and there is no doubt, we are certainly in a different situation right now. The answer is to apply the basics as described in this book but also adopt an inspired, creative and fresh approach to getting the business.

In a McGraw-Hill study of over 600 businesses it emerged that during a recession, aggressive advertisers increased their market share by 2.5 times the average of non-recession advertisers. In 1981-2, businesses that continued to advertise during the downturn generated higher than average sales growth in the three years that followed. Fascinatingly, during the boom of 2001, 80% of businesses increased their advertising spend, which yielded little or no increase in market share. This was simply because everyone had increased spend and the markets had reached saturation.

YouGov '08 research shows that businesses are is less concerned about the economy, business rates and regulations than they are about the competition. This highlights the key point that there has never been a better opportunity to capture new customers from your competitors, and that now is the time to increase communication and not reduce it.

A quote from A.G. Lafley, the Chairman and CEO of Procter & Gamble, underpins this strategy:

"I think it's more essential to innovate through a recession and certainly what we're trying to do at P&G is continue to bring sustaining and even disruptive new brands and products for our consumers, to make their lives better, to offer them a little more value."

If we are able to be innovative in the way we sell advertising, clients will listen, and that increases our chance of selling something. The above quote suggests the P&G approach may include creating 'disruptive brands' which suggests they want to bring about change to both purchasing patterns and the way their customers are thinking about the products. Perception is everything. If clients perceive advertising as pure expenditure as opposed to an investment in long-term growth then selling space it is going to be extremely difficult.

There are three things you need to do in a sales call if faced with this objection, to avoid it ending too soon. The first is to agree with the client that reviewing advertising expenditure is the right approach. Now that this is no longer an issue of difference, the next step is to introduce a new problem – one we can solve. This is supported by the third element, which is to imply the potential loss of existing customers if all advertising is stopped. You will also need to think creatively, rely on your natural persuasiveness and apply the techniques provided in this book.

My advice on how to sell advertising through a recession is based on these principles. Media salespeople, irrespective of whether they have experienced a recession, need to grasp the point that downturns provide the opportunity to widen the gap between competitors. Hiding-under-the-duvet marketing isn't going to work in the long run and defines a false economy. If we can persuade even 5% of non-recession advertisers to rethink their strategy then we will, in our own way, kick-start the beginning of recovery.

Koko was made in London and available between 1888 and was still available in 1915. Claims included preventing hair loss or premature greying as well as the "eradication of scurf" which is helpful (whatever scurf is). Interestingly, the British Medical Association concluded it was 94% water and contained alcohol and formaldehyde, which is very useful if you feel the need to pickle your thatch.

Part 5

Conclusion

"Luck is what happens when preparation meets opportunity."

Seneca

17. A final word

I started this book by talking about the provenance of the media sales role. I explained how the start of magazine publishing in the 1850s marked the beginning of the information revolution that continues today. The media industry has changed significantly since those days and indeed, it's changed quite a lot since last year. In many ways, that represents the nature of the business, forever changing.

In my opinion, the downturn has dramatically increased the reliance media owners place on their salespeople. The tenacity and imagination of media sales professionals has never been more central to an organisation's future success. Salespeople are known for their ability to communicate, persuade and influence and now is the time to step up to the mark.

The job teaches the skills needed in practically every senior management position in the country. Ask anyone what makes a good leader and people will say 'he talks to everyone irrespective of status' or 'she listens to our ideas' or 'they motivate, inspire and encourage us', all of which are communication skills, which is just what this job teaches.

Selling advertising space is an extremely worthwhile occupation that teaches the skills we need in every area of social and business life. It is an accessible career, too, with plenty of companies offering roles at this level to both graduates and non-graduates. It has a discernable career progression and for those with proven skills can provide a quite exceptional standard of living. Publishing is also a very sociable business with a great many like-minded folk ending up friends in life as well as at work. Many of us who have been in the business for a number of years are still in touch with people we met when we first started out as trainees.

It is also an industry that is by its very nature ever-changing. The internet has revolutionised global communications and opened up undiscovered markets in a way that hasn't been seen since the commercialisation of television the 1950s. The internet is still under-developed and will inevitably become faster, more accessible, interactive, accountable and generally media-dominant in the years ahead.

That is not to suggest that the web will replace magazines – far from it. As I said in the first part of the book, our world has an unquenchable thirst for information and whatever your message, be it commercial, social, religious or just plain amusing, the more ways to share it the better.

That's advertising.

18. Glossary of terms

Ad Banner
One of the terms used to describe an image or media object on a website for the purpose of promoting a product or service. There are also other expressions relating to different styles on online advertisements such as Skyscrapers and pop-ups.

Advertisement copy
Copy refers to the client's advertisement. The client may submit the copy in any number of formats. It can be attached to an email in final form as a pdf or jpeg file and sent to the production department. Advertisement copy can also be produced by publishing houses in most cases and this helps advertisers commit as they have no further work or costs to consider.

Advertisement space
The area in a magazine or on a website that is used to publish messages from paying advertisers.

Assumptive close
The strength of the relationship and how well the sale is going will determine whether an assumptive close is appropriate. A salesperson using an assumptive close avoids actually asking the client if they would like to proceed and instead takes for granted that they would like to book.

Audit Bureau of Circulation
An independent organisation that provides detailed analysis of a magazine's circulation. It can include a breakdown of reader category and regional information.

Benefit

Following on from a feature, a benefit is precisely what the specific client to whom the salesperson is talking will receive as a result of buying. Benefits should provide the solution to the identified needs.

Bimonthly

Confusingly, this can mean two things. A bimonthly magazine may be published every two months or twice a month (sometimes referred to as fortnightly).

BOM

An acronym that stands for Background Objective Method. It is a suggested guide to those looking to probe customers for information. B builds rapport and asks non-challenging questions, O allows us to understand more about what they are trying to achieve and M ascertains their planned activity.

Business to business (b2b)

A business that sells products or provides services to other businesses. In publishing houses, this term is used to describe the type of product. A b2b magazine is one that provides business information to those operating in a specified market. It is the transference of information and services from one business to another without the involvement of the consumer.

Button

A clickable image or object featured on a website. Often advertisers use this to encourage customers to click through to their own website.

Call log sheet

One of the key performance indicators in media sales is the volume of calls made per day, against target. A call log is simply a method to record how many outgoing calls are being made and whether or not they were effective calls.

Call rates

This is a term used to describe how many telephone sales calls salespeople are making each day.

Checking questions

Used at the end of the questioning section of a sales call by the salesperson to find out if there is anything that has not been discussed that may have a bearing on a future proposal.

Circulation

In the magazine publishing industry, this refers to the amount of copies printed.

Classified or Entry Level media sales executive

A job within a publishing house that has primary responsibility for the sale of advertisement space to prospective advertisers.

Click-through-rate (CTR)

Cost of an action taken by a visitor to a website. Advertising is sometimes sold on the basis of a CTR which means there is no agreed total amount but a smaller amount paid each time a visitor clicks on the advertisement. These smaller amounts can build up and become quite expensive. The other problem is that it re-focuses the attention of the advertiser on the price as opposed to the value. As we know, advertising *influences* customers and this cannot be measured purely by the volume of direct action.

Client record system

Every sales operation has to have a system to record client interaction. This will hold key data such as contact details, past activity as well as brief notes on calls or meetings experienced with the client.

Close
The final part of the sales process. Once the needs have been identified and matched, asking for the order follows. Closing means closing the deal. However, try to think of closing as something that starts the moment you begin talking to a prospect.

Closed questions
Used a good deal in conversation, these are questions that can receive only a 'yes' or a 'no' answer. These are only helpful if you need either a yes or a no!

Competencies
The skills and personal attributes required for a role. Some are essential and others are desirable and some can be learned while others are innate. These are often used as the basis to questions at interview to assess candidates. They should also appear on the job description to ensure expectations are understood and to provide further clarity about the requirements of the job function.

Competitors
Companies that vie for a share of the sector revenue in the same market.

Confirmations
As each feature and benefit is described, salespeople should get the client to agree to the value of the solution described. This is useful to the salesperson as the more agreement we receive along the way, the less likely we are to face an objection.

Consumer
In the context of publishing, a consumer magazine or website is one intended to be read by the general public as opposed to businesspeople.

Credit Control

After you sell the space and the advertisement appears, the invoice is sent. Advertisers then have a period of time to pay, usually thirty days. Once this period lapses, this department of well trained and skilled individuals will contact the debtor and chase the money. It is important for media salespeople to be in touch with this department and to know who pays on time, which companies pay up but pay late and who the non-payers might be. The old adage of 'a sale isn't a sale until it's paid for' is as important today as it's ever been.

Customer/client/advertiser

These all mean the same thing. They describe an individual or a company that either already advertises or may in the future.

Cut-off/deadline

All sales operations have deadlines and publishing is no exception. To reach the cut-off or deadline on a media-related product means the period of selling has stopped. For example a weekly magazine may 'close' on Wednesday at 3pm. This means selling on that issue must cease by then as it has to go to the printers to be published.

Decision-maker

This refers to a client who has the seniority to decide whether or not to advertise with a media owner. A media sales executive will aim to speak to as many decision-makers as possible in order to close deals. It can also refer to the quality of readership. If a magazine or website reaches KDMs (key decision-makers) it is more useful to advertisers.

Decisional questions

Questions that help us work out when a sale is likely to occur. They include finding out who is responsible for placing bookings and how long it usually takes for decisions to be made.

Demographic
A word that refers to selected characteristics within a population. It groups people by certain criteria. A mainstream consumer publication for example, would be aimed at high-income house owners aged 26-34 living in the central and southern parts of the UK. This is a demographic.

Direct mail
A form of media whereby companies that wish to advertise use a list of named individuals to send their message to. This can be done by using the postal system or through email.

Dwell-time
Information derived from the server to measure how long viewers or users are looking at a web page or website. This information is amongst quite a bit of data usually provided to media sales teams by the web operations department.

Effective call
Definitions of an effective call vary. Basically an effective call is one where a salesperson has got through to the key decision-maker and has, at the very least, managed to talk about one or two benefits of the product.

Feature
An indisputable fact about a product being sold. Features of a product help to indicate why it might be an ideal place to advertise.

Frequency
A term relating to how often a magazine is published. For example, the frequency of *The Guardian* is daily, whereas *Marketing Week* is produced weekly and *Tatler* is monthly.

Gatekeepers
Employees at client companies whose role includes the protection of senior personnel from unwanted phone calls.

Illustrative close
An illustrative close means the salesperson enables a prospective client to imagine either what his advertisement may look like if he were to proceed or how he would react if he were to receive a lot of interest from new customers. This helps to close deals in the cases where clients are finding it difficult to visualise a result.

Impulse buys
These are products that are bought without the need for much thought.

Influence
The main purpose to advertising. As advertised solutions are very often protracted purchases (see definition later on), advertising is maintained to influence customers through their research.

Key performance indicators (KPI)
Often to be found listed on a job description. A KPI is specific to a job role and is the measure by which employee performance can be judged. For example, the volume of sales is a KPI for a media salesperson, as is the number of calls made.

Leads and lead chasing
Leads refer to potential areas where business can be expected. A lead is a customer who may not yet have been contacted, but for whom there are indications they may want to buy advertising space. Lead chasing within a publishing house means a salesperson is perhaps scouring the competition to see if there is anyone they should call to get business. The search for prospective business includes looking at magazines, websites and attending live events.

Linked questions

These are closed questions aimed at finding out whether a client is interested in achieving what we know we can provide. They are used during the early part of the sale and before we have told them the benefits of our product.

List rental/e-list rental

Companies wishing to send an advertising message using direct mail do so either by having developed their own lists of potential customers or by renting a list from a media owner. List rental is a lucrative revenue stream for a publishing house. The names are often taken from the list of magazine subscribers who have declared interest in receiving relevant material from a third party. Additionally, companies can buy lists of email addresses if they wish to send their advertising message electronically.

Marketplace/directory/index/suppliers update

Examples of titles given to various sections within the classified advertisement section of magazines.

Market share

This term relates to the measurement of how a product compares against the market in general. For example a consumer magazine may have secured 200 advertisement pages during a quarter. If we added up all the advertisement pages sold by all the competitive magazines during the same period and divided one by another, we would find out our market share. We can work out a market share on revenue too, by estimating prices paid for the same number of pages. It's a simple comparison that helps Publishers see how they are doing in their respective markets.

Marketing plan

A prepared plan covering perhaps a year, developed by companies to promote their product or service within their sector. This may include developing a website, press or direct mail advertising and attendance at exhibitions.

Match
The second part of the sales process. When we match, we are explaining how our product matches the identified needs. We match by using Features and Benefits.

Media
Any channel that can be used to advertise a product or service. These range from TV, radio, mobile phones, newspapers and magazines, posters, websites, conferences, exhibitions and direct mail to the backs of buses.

Media owner
Any company that is control of the above, such as a TV or radio station, a publishing house or an exhibitions company.

Needs
This term is applied in media sales to the facts we gather from clients illustrating what they want to achieve.

News-stand copy sales
As well as being sold via subscription or on a controlled free distribution, magazines are also sold in newsagents and this term refers to this activity.

On target earnings (OTE)
Refers to the potential commission salespeople can earn. Commissions will be paid based on how well the individual or team have done against a preset target.

Open questions
A question that extracts more than a 'yes' or 'no' answer, usually

prefixed by Who, What, Where, How, Why or When.

Optional close
A salesperson can avoid asking questions that will simply elicit a yes or no and ask if a customer would prefer to take one option or another. This way they will consider which is more appropriate rather than whether or not they should advertise at all.

Page impression or page view /hit
A measurement of response from a user to a specific web page. The retrieval of any item, like a page or a graphic, from a web server. However, if the page retrieved from the web features a number of graphics, the number of hits or page impressions recorded is one for the entire page and one for each graphic. Therefore it is not a good indication of web traffic.

Pausing
This follows asking for commitment with a closing question such as "Would you like to go ahead with the series of 52 insertions at the price discussed?" A pause is when salespeople, having applied the sales structure, await the client's reply. It gives the client time to think about whether they should proceed or not.

Personalisation strategies
An ever-increasing application to internet marketing, this makes the identification of users far more accurate, which makes real-time user recognition achievable.

Portfolio Selling
A new term describing the sale of more than one media. For media salespeople, this is usually restricted to online and print advertisement sales but for display, this can extend to sponsorship and events.

Price objection
An opinion or view the client has as to why he believes the space he has been offered is too expensive.

Probe
The first and most important part of the sales process. Probe means to investigate, dig deep and find out as much as you can about a client's needs.

Production
This department is responsible for putting a magazine together. Production staff co-ordinate all the advertising copy and editorial together to provide the printers with the correct material to be able to produce the finished magazine on time.

Production book
The production book is a dated record of all advertisers, revenue levels and copy requirements of every issue. This is either paper or electronic but acts as a centralised resource for all those involved.

Profit v loss close
A close that helps us illustrate the financial implications of *not* doing something. Can they afford not to advertise? How would it impact on the overall profitability if, for example, they didn't acquire enough new business?

Protracted buy
A product that is bought following extensive research, analysis and discussion perhaps over quite a long time.

Puppy dog close
A close that means we ask them for the business for little other reason than it will make our day! In this case, we hope they sympathise and give us their money.

Rapport

Crucial to every client/salesperson relationship, rapport is the understanding, affinity or connection we have with others. Salespeople have to build relationships with customers and being able to get along with most people is an important attribute for salespeople at all levels.

Rebound close

This is less of a close and more of a technique to deflect a difficult question. If a client asks about the cost of advertising too early in the call, we can respond by asking them how many they were thinking of buying, or that costs are hard to work out until we know more about their precise needs. They may decide to take it no further if they are aware of the price before the benefits.

Recruitment agency

A recruitment agency is employed by a company looking to fill one or more vacancies. Their responsibilities include receiving the remit from the client for the post or posts they wish to fill, creating a suitable advertisement and then contacting the publishing houses to negotiate advertisement rates. An agency buys the space but anyone wishing to apply for the position should apply directly to the recruiting client and not the agency. A media sales executive looking to work in the recruitment advertisement sales department will contact these companies.

Recruitment consultancy

A company working on behalf of clients with job vacancies. They place the advertising where they believe they will get the best response and the applicants reply directly to them. They are acting as a middleman between the applicant and the recruiting company to help with the legwork associated to the recruitment process, adding a good deal of selection and interview experience and skill.

Rejection
A term used in publishing referring to the point at which a potential advertiser has declined the offer to advertise.

Response rate
The volume of interest a published advertisement generates from the readership.

Revenue stream
The origination of revenue. For example, advertisements, subscriptions and copy sales are all revenue streams for publishing houses. Areas from which revenue can be derived.

Sales targets
Salespeople are given an amount of revenue to generate within a specified time and this is a sales target.

Subscriptions
A subscription is an important revenue stream for publishing houses. It means an individual has made an upfront payment to the media owner in order to receive either a magazine or full access to a website.

Summary
A summary in the context of media sales refers to the point at which the salesperson repeats the main needs extracted from the Probing part of the sale. A summary is a useful tool to bring the conversation back to the sale and also to ensure nothing is missed or misinterpreted.

Time management
A general business term that relates to how we manage the time we have to achieve the preset and agreed goals.

Trade
In the context of the media, a trade magazine provides information for blue-collar industries such as grocery, manufacturing, retail and engineering. A business magazine will reach those that are key decision-makers, while a trade magazine will go to the technicians. A consumer magazine reaches the end user made up of a specific demographic.

Unique user
This is a more reliable measure of interest generated by a website and refers to the number of different users who view a website within a certain time period. This is different from the number of hits, since each user could visit more than once. To identify unique users, a user registration or identification system is required.

Yield
This refers to the amount of revenue that has to be achieved to make the required profit. If a magazine has to generate £10,000 and has ten pages of advertising, then each page has a yield of £1,000. The figure of £10,000 takes into account general costs and the required profit level.

Zoo
A place where they keep animals.

19. Media Sales – FAQ

I've read your book and I'm interested in media sales. Where do I begin?

Two routes – you can contact a few publishing houses direct. They often have a 'jobs' field on their websites and an opportunity to upload your CV with a covering letter explaining your desire to get into media sales. Or you could find some media specialist recruitment agencies online. These companies will give you a great deal more information on your choices, provide excellent guidance and support and hopefully line you up with a few interviews.

What's the difference between selling advertisement space for a digital, consumer or business product?

The application of the sales process explained in this book can be used across all media. So in principle, there is no difference to the technical skill of selling space. The differences lie in what we ask, the solutions we offer and how it is measured. In fact, discussing online as a marketing solution with buyers can be complex. It is, however, probably the most fascinating and challenging area available, not least because it's still in its infancy.

What's the social life like?

Really good. As most people at entry-level media sales are in their twenties, the social life tends to revolve around the fun stuff like pubs, restaurants and clubs. Companies also arrange team days or summer sports events and even sports teams that play inter-company and industry leagues.

How much chocolate can I expect to eat?

Quite a lot although it's not compulsory. Media sales staff are known to consumer more biscuits, cake and chocolate than any other industry in the western hemisphere.

What's the best – b2b consumer or online?
No answer to this. I've done all of them and quite honestly, it's more about the people. The most important thing is to get into a company that has an excellent training provision, excellent brands to work on and to try to get into a growing or stable market.

What will my friends say when I tell them I've got a job in media sales?
They will want to be like you.

What time do you start work?
9am or 9.30 depending and then you can go home at 5.30pm. You get an hour for lunch. Some departments require you to work a bit later particularly if you are dealing with overseas clients or on a tough deadline.

Can I use media sales to get into marketing or journalism?
More vacancies within media sales emerge than in other areas of the business and the skills you learn in media sales are hugely transferable to other business areas. I wouldn't recommend this route but as long as you are prepared to commit heart and soul at entry-level media sales for a year at least, then I suppose there's nothing wrong with it. You may even get tempted to stay!

Is there any travel?
Unlikely in the first couple of years but again, it depends on the market.

Do I get to meet clients?
Not early on. However, there will be opportunities to attend various functions or events associated to the market you work in as well as potential to go with your manager on meetings.

Will I find the partner of my dreams in media sales?
Maybe.

Will I be able to use Facebook or Bebo while selling media space?
No. This is work.

What's the training in?
Sales training includes a basic sales module on what it's all about then progressing to other modules on negotiation, online selling, advanced selling, writing proposals and presentation skills. This should be delivered either by an external specialist or internal training department. Avoid succumbing to promises of training that ends up being fifteen minutes with the manager every three months – it's worth nothing.

What are the company benefits usually on offer?
These vary. Usually benefits include shop discounts, pension schemes, savings and share plans, health insurance plans. Most of these will be available after probation.

I've lost my house key, do you know where it is?
Yes.

How soon after starting will I begin to earn commission?
I can't answer this with any real accuracy. All I can say is your employer will want you to start selling as soon as possible and consequently you will earn commission, so it will be sooner rather than later. Although it might be wise to anticipate low commission earning early on that will grow the better you become at the job.

You're book is fantastic.
Thanks.

20. References

Books

Guerrilla Negotiating, Levinson Smith Wilson (Wiley, 1999)

Selling by Phone, Linda Richards (McGraw Hill, 1992)

IDS Compensation Review (Income Data Services)

Websites

b2bmedia.co.uk

bbc.co.uk

dotprint.com

SearchCIO.com

victorianweb.org

Organisations

Interactive Advertising Bureau (IAB)

Periodical Publishers Association

Round 8 Recruitment

Sift Media

The UK Association of Online Publishers (AOP)

YouGov